AF594188

Davenport's Version

A Narrative Poem

John Gery

Book Design by Sarah T. Travis

Acknowledgements: Thanks to the following museums for permission to use images from paintings in their collections: Front cover image from "Farragut's Fleet Passing the Forts Below New Orleans" by Mauritz Frederick De Haas, ca. 1866, Williams Research Center, Historic New Orleans Collection; back cover image from "Pontchartain Beach" by John Genin, ca. 1870, New Orleans Museum of Art; "Giant Steamboats on the Levee at New Orleans" by Hippolyte Sebron, 1853, Newcomb Art Department of Tulane University; "Maison Ponchartrain Nouvelle Orleans" by Nicolino Calyo, 1848, Ogden Museum of Southern Art, University of New Orleans; "Bayou Plaquemines" by Joseph Rusling Meeker, 1881, Ogden Museum of Southern Art; "Bayou Sunset" by Harold Rudolph, 1871, New Orleans Museum of Art; "Battle of Port Hudson on the Mississippi" by Edward Everard Arnold, 1864, Louisiana State University Museum of Art, Baton Rouge.

Passages from Book I of *Davenport's Version*, in different versions, appeared in *Louisiana Literature*. A chapbook of an earlier version of Parts 1-6 of Book IV received the Charles Williams Duke Long Poem Award from Amelia Press and was published as *The Burning of New Orleans* (Bakersfield, CA, 1988). Grateful acknowledgements to the editors of these publications for their support.

Portals Press
4411 Fontainebleau Drive
New Orleans, Louisiana USA 70125

Library of Congress Cataloging-in-Publication Data

Gery, John.
Davenport's Version : narrative poem / John Gery.
p. cm.
ISBN 0-916620-58-1
1. New Orleans (La.)--History--Civil War, 1861-1865--Poetry
2. New Orleans (La.)--Poetry. 3. Reconstruction--Poetry. I. Title.
PS3557.E745 D38 2003
811' .54--dc21

20022151015

Contents

A Brief History of the Poem

Whiles others fish with craft for great opinion,
I with great truth catch mere simplicity.
Shakespeare's Troilus

As a poet and teacher with a modest reputation in this city, I am sometimes visited by poets and other literary aficionados seeking an audience. Usually, like pilgrims carrying their meager oblations to a presbyter, these writers come to my office with tales of woe or poems of heartbreak, and just by listening to them unburden themselves for half an hour I can alleviate, at least temporarily, any urgency they have about actually displaying their writing. After a quiet conversation, in which I try to impress on them the rigors of making art, I never hear from them again.

The case of this manuscript, however, was an exception. Some time ago, as I was sitting idly in my office at the university, a thin, pallid but neatly groomed man appeared at my door and introduced himself. At first I assumed from his dark suit and polished shoes that he was either a book salesman or book buyer seeking discarded desk copies of textbooks; although he was only about thirty, he had wispy, greying hair, with his only distinguishing trait a periodic tic in his right shoulder. After I invited him to sit, he began nervously to explain that he had been directed to me by one of my colleagues who had assured him I was always interested in poets and loved talking with them about their work. Then he quickly added that he himself knew nothing about poetry and was, in fact, afraid of literature. He'd had a few English courses in college, but that had been long ago and in another city.

As he sat there talking, I casually waved to another colleague sauntering by my open office door — a gesture which caused this man to spin around abruptly, as though he feared the passerby might recognize him. Then he turned back and, his face now as white as a blank page, asked in a tremor, "Is this a bad time for you?" I said it was as good a time as ever and encouraged him to continue.

In a low voice, almost a whisper, and with some deliberation as though to avoid grammatical errors, he explained that he worked as a teller at the First National Trust of Commerce on Canal Street downtown, "and," he added with a twitch of his shoulder, "I live in the French Quarter." I said that I, too, lived there, had in fact for a decade, and so wondered whether he and I might have met somewhere before — at a party, perhaps. His twitching shoulder dropped in relief but he assured me we hadn't, so I nodded, then glanced, vaguely, at my watch.

After a pause, he resumed talking. For no reason he knew of, in his job at the bank, he had, over a period of several months, become the unwilling subject of a particular client's attention. Apparently, once each week, an older man (somewhere between sixty and ninety, but he couldn't say) would come to his window to make small withdrawals or deposits from his savings account, never adding up to more than a few dollars either way. This man, as the teller described him, had a scruffy beard and hunched back, and he wasn't very tall; always dressed in the same light brown clothes that were too big for him, especially his pants held up by suspenders and rolled at the ankles, the man nonetheless carried a well-pressed jacket over his left arm. Each time he came to the window he would smile at the teller and ask after his health, in an accent not exactly Southern, not exactly Cajun, not exactly anything, though not exactly not anything either.

As the weeks passed, the teller began to notice the old man letting others in line go ahead of him to the other windows, preferring always to wait until his own window was free. "I didn't think much of it at first," he whispered to me, "I figured I reminded the old man of his son or somebody." Then one Friday afternoon, after withdrawing another small sum for the man, the teller carefully balanced his records for the week and exited through the bank's massive oaken doors onto Canal Street. There outside, lingering behind one of the great grey concrete columns and now puttering toward him, was the old man, his jacket still draped over his left arm, with a handkerchief for wiping the sweat from his face clutched in one hand. After asking about his health, the old man grabbed the teller's elbow, leaned into him and, leering up at him with a semi-toothless grin, invited him back to his "rooms" in the French Quarter. He wanted to show him something.

At this point in his story, the teller averted his eyes from me but continued speaking. "I've certainly been approached on the street before," he said, his shoulder giving a twitch, "that's not why I'm telling you this."

"What happened?" I asked.

The teller paused, looked up at the crumbling tiles in my office ceiling, and laughed. "Since I was headed in that direction anyway — you know, home — I figured why not humor the old codger. I've read those stories about Howard Hughes and other rich people who live like hobos, then die and leave their millions to strangers they happened to meet on the street. I decided to go with him, at least part way."

He then described their journey down Canal Street to Chartres, where they turned into the Quarter and walked a few blocks to a small entry between a toy soldier shop and one of those barely noticeable restaurants called Tom's Oyster House or Sam's. Here the old man pulled a rusting iron key from his pocket and unlocked the narrow door onto a damp stone gutter running the length of both buildings. The two men squeezed through this passage into a tiny courtyard, where half a dozen garbage cans were stacked against the back wall of the restaurant, crossed the open space to the rear, and climbed two flights on a rickety wooden staircase up an old square building with a long balcony and French doors.

"The smell of garlic and fish entrails was overwhelming," the teller could not keep himself from adding, "but once we entered his rooms, that smell gave way to the stink of his belongings — mildewed curtains that dragged across the floor when he opened the doors, an ancient couch that converted to his bed, an old rolltop desk with a chair whose slats were missing. He obviously never dusted or cleaned anything." His shoulder twitched again, as he added, "Anyway, he didn't lock the doors when we came in, so I figured there was no danger. And he acted so kindly toward me."

Once inside the old man stepped to a stone fireplace, whose mantle was higher than his hunched shoulders. On the wall above it hung a black and white drawing of a young woman. From the mantle he pulled down a bottle and two small glasses. What he poured into them he swore was pure absinthe, the kind that hasn't been legal in Louisiana for decades. To the teller it tasted like a combination of licorice and linseed oil. I remember how his tongue shot out of his mouth as he told me this.

But then, suddenly, my telephone rang. It was my associate dean asking me to come upstairs to his office immediately to consult on an urgent matter concerning my pending review for promotion. For the teller's sake, I disguised my alarm at the tone of the associate dean's voice.

After I hung up, the teller sprang to his feet and said in a loud voice, "I'm sorry. I shouldn't bother you with any of this."

"No, no," I tried to assure him, "I have a minute, or two. Finish." I glanced at my watch.

With his shoulder now jerking intermittently, he explained how after a second glass of absinthe the old man pointed to the sketch above the fireplace and referred to it as his proudest possession. "The woman in it, she couldn't have been more than twenty," the teller told me. "She was sickly, thin — you know, like those portraits that hang in the museums on Jackson Square? The old man claimed she was some relative of his, I think, or maybe his former lover. Then he gave me the kind of look a fortune teller gives you right before telling you you'll inherit a million dollars. He walked over to his desk drawer and brought out a pile of tattered papers. At first he mumbled something about finding it in the attic of his uncle's house somewhere — who knows? — but then he thrust it at me and said he wanted me to have it, to read it and take care of it for him. He kind of smiled at me strangely and just said I would know what to do with it. I wanted to ask, *why would I?* but I was a little scared of him. You know, he was *very* serious about it."

I rose from my chair. "And?" I asked.

"I hoped that, well, I figured you might like to read that manuscript. It's a long poem and well, seeing as you like poetry, I thought it might interest you, that you might, you know, look it over. Then you can tell me if it's worth anything. The old man, he's gone now. He either died, moved away or something, and here I am with his property. I'm afraid to have it around, a little. I don't know what to do with it." He stood and glanced nervously out my door.

Quickly, I explained I already had other manuscripts to read, lots of them, and that at that particular moment I needed to go to an urgent meeting, but if he were to bring me his manuscript I might glance at it. I couldn't promise when, given how busy I was, and I tried to suggest that I doubted its worth (though, of course, I equivocated in case it was actually written by him, as I didn't want to insult him). After all, I added as usual, poetry is a rigorous and difficult art that takes years to cultivate. From his frown I guessed that without being unkind I had nonetheless sufficiently discouraged him from returning. We parted without shaking hands, and it was only on my way upstairs that I realized I had already forgotten his name.

Sometime later I received in the mail a large brown envelope with no return address on it. Inside, to my chagrin, was the very manuscript the teller had described, printed out by hand on hundreds of faded sheets of what looked like old official stationery or government contract paper. It seemed well-preserved, but I couldn't tell for certain how old it was: in this city, if you do not keep personal papers in a dry, enclosed space, the humid air soon begins to corrode them. What the teller had sent me may have been anywhere from a decade to more than a hundred years old. It being an especially busy day for me, I shoved the manuscript onto a shelf between other unsolicited papers, thinking to get back to it later, just in case he might call.

There it remained for, I guess, a year. The teller never reappeared. In fact, I had completely forgotten about him until one August day, alone in my office, I sat sweating unsuccessfully over a short poem I planned to submit to a leading literary journal in the Midwest. As on most summer afternoons here, it was unbearably hot, and my mind kept drifting to a discussion I had had that morning with the associate dean about my faltering status on the faculty; it seemed my scholarly output did not really suit the future direction of the college, as he saw it. Out of frustration, I threw my pen down and stared at the paint peeling off my office walls. Then, spotting the teller's manuscript bulging beneath a pile of ignored papers like a brick about to come loose, I yanked it out and began idly to leaf through it.

I admit at first I was scornful. How is it, I thought, that I who have spent years writing poetry can't manage to produce even a few publishable lines, while illiterates like that bank teller have no trouble pouring out page after page of verse, without the least bit of self-consciousness? But then I started to adjust to the steady pace of the long poem, and the more I read, the more I began to suspect that what the teller had told me was not such a hoax after all.

Since that fortuitous afternoon I've had no luck in locating either the teller or the old man he said had given him the manuscript, which I have decided on my own to call *Davenport's Version*. I have investigated the names used in it and have discovered that at least some of them belonged to people who actually lived here in the 1860s, during and after the Federal occupation. Where the story originated, whether there was a Northerner named David Davenport stationed here, and at what point he spent what was obviously considerable energy composing this poem "in straight lines" remain so far unanswered questions. Furthermore, to my knowledge, no authorized record of a Bressie LaRouché, the poem's central figure, exists; maybe whoever wrote the poem has falsified her name for irrecoverable, private reasons, or maybe her history has simply been erased.

For my part, I have tried not to interfere with the poem more than I thought necessary. I have regularized spellings and cleared up whatever seemed to me confusing. I also found among the papers, scratched in a handwriting different from that of the manuscript itself, an excerpt copied from a letter by Lafcadio Hearn to his friend H.E. Krehbiel, where that somewhat mystical author describes his "ancient dream of a poetical prose -- compositions to satisfy an old Greek ear — like chants wrought in huge measure, wider than the widest line of a Sanskrit composition, and just a little irregular, like Ocean-rhythm." "I fancy," this fragment continues, "that I shall have produced a pleasant effect on the reader's mind, simply with pictures; and that the secret work, the word-work, will not be noticed for its own sake." I also found two other epigraphs, which I have attached, though they, too, may have alternate sources.

Maybe one day someone will locate that black and white sketch of the young woman that hung above the fireplace in the old man's French Quarter rooms. There, I believe, lies the key to the mystery behind this poem. In the meantime, I accept responsibility only for what is attributed to me. As some poet said once, "Truth is a thing that ever I will keep"; the rest is someone else's.

...every kyndely thyng that is
Hath a kyndely stede ther he
May best in hyt conserved be;
Unto which place everythyng,
Thorgh his kyndely enclynyng,
Moveth for to come to,
Whan that hyt is awey therfro....
And for this cause mayst thou see
That every ryver to the see
Enclyned ys to goo by kynde.

— Chaucer, *The House of Fame*

The final wall of the wise man's thought however is Human Kindness of course. If the road of disappointment, grief, pessimism, is followed far enough, it will arrive there. Pessimism itself is only a little, little way, and moreover it is ridiculously cheap. The cynical mind is an uneducated thing. Therefore do I strive to be as kind and as just as may be to those about me and in my meagre success at it, I find the solitary pleasure in life.

— Stephen Crane in a letter to Nellie Crouse

Davenport's Version

DAVENPORT'S VERSION

BOOK I

1

I sing of fidelity and kindness.
You who years from now may chance to find this,
grant me grace to get things right.

Return now
to the War Between the States. At Bull Run
(later called the Battle of Manassas)
Congressmen came out to watch the fighting.
Wealthy families skipped church, packed baskets,
and dressed up their children for a picnic.
Someone put up bleachers near the hillside
where the spectacle was to unfold.
No one arrived late, and most came early,
not as they would to a church recital
or another speech about secession.
Under cloudless skies, the day was mild
for July, so drivers of barouches
flipped their tops down, gentlemen doffed boaters,
ladies brought their parasols, and children,
being children, left their hats at home.
As they rode down dusty Warrenton Turnpike,
through them came McDowell's Union Army
marching cheerfully toward Manassas.
But before they'd started out that morning,
Beauregard had placed his troops near Stone Bridge,
Johnston had come up from Shenandoah
on a train, and Jackson and his graycoats
had bivouacked by the wall that'd make him famous.

Morning passed. The air was cool and pleasant.
After lunching on cold breasts of chicken,
boiled eggs, goat cheese, and golden apples,
served with burgundy, the gay onlookers,
squinting from the bright sun, saw their heroes
in the distance, as they crossed the river
over Stone Bridge and up Henry House Hill.
Each corps flashed the colors of its home state —
red for Massachusetts volunteers,

green for those from Pennsylvania, purple
for the New York 7th's "silken stockings."
From afar they looked like quilted patchwork
but ten minutes later, when the guns popped
and men started dropping to the road bed,
it appeared as though a giant cat's paws
tore that quilt apart from underneath it.
Blood they couldn't see, not from that distance,
only caps, or heads, blown off — or arms flung,
pulled this way and that. All afternoon
General McDowell of the Union
ordered onslaught after heavy onslaught,
forcing back the rebels, then reporting,
"Victory is ours! The war is over!"

He was wrong, of course, once reinforcements,
Johnston's men, as green as their dead comrades,
rushed in by surprise, fresh from Manassas.
Crouched behind the bodies of the fallen,
using them to shield themselves from crossfire,
they took shots at everything in sight —
bluecoats, horses, Congressmen, sunflowers,
Mrs. Henry propped up in her kitchen
like a statue. Some already wounded
were shot at again, and in that chaos
children lost their parents, ladies panicked,
running wild with skirts above their knees,
gentlemen took off into the forests
and weren't seen for days, and even soldiers
who'd enlisted for three months of service
opted suddenly to take their first leave.
"We" had lost the "Battle of Manassas"
(also called the "Battle of Bull Run"),
21 Jul. 1861.

2

South of Market Street in Philadelphia
in a cool and breezy upstairs tea room,
sitting with a girl who'd just turned twenty,
I read through the *New York Herald*'s story
of Manassas. This was three days later.
Then I turned and signaled for the waiter.

3

I'm a casual reader, no historian,
so my memory for details falters.
That's why I am writing this in straight lines,
hoping they will help me to remember
only what's important. What's important?
Stories, music, getting up on time,
details such as what we ate for breakfast
after our first night together, the names.
Poetry does best by making small things
matter, unknown persons join the living,
simple gestures otherwise forgotten
dance like light on water — or does nothing.
Like Prometheus' entrails ripped by vultures
or the limbs of Hector dragged by horses,
tales of war are grand stuff in the telling
more than in the history they come from.
Bodies always end up merely bodies.
My tale has the telling only, nothing
else, no heroes, no triumphant nations,
no immortal acts or famous speeches.
They're recorded elsewhere in the great books,
epic verse, and military annals
written by those men who understand war
better than I do. Look at those sources
for a full account of how "The South" broke —
after years of bitter aggravation —
from "The Union," from the legislation
of those "Northern hangmen" who were "strangling"
their economy and way of life.
In Virginia, both the Carolinas
and the "Deep South" as they call where I am,
men were no more "anti-democratic"
than was Pericles, that ancient father
of equality — that's what they argued:
Look at Europe! Aren't there lowborns there, too,
who in all but race resemble Negroes?
They, too, work for masters who protect them,
feed them, clothe them, care for them in sickness,
never bother them with money matters
(which, experience proves, would just corrupt them),
and provide them meaningful employment?

In return, these masters only ask them
to be honest and to be devoted
to their Christian principles and faith.
Certainly, some planters do abuse them,
mostly to increase their profits; money
has betrayed them. But the god of money,
for which slaves have little need, is worshipped
in the North, as though to enter heaven
one were measured by his bank account.
You demand an individual's price;
we protect an individual's rights.

Abolition! was the Northern answer,
No one shall control another's freedom!
And to war this argument would lead them.

4

But before you think that I'm a tortoise
plodding over old ground for no purpose —
I'm more like the loris, if you know him,
creature of the night, wide-eyed and skinny,
quiet, not particularly observant,
and slow, though not lethargic — I'll get started:

Charles LaRouché was born a Creole
in New Orleans. But his French-born father,
following Louisiana custom,
sent his son north for an education.
It was 1824, the same year
Byron caught his death at Missolonghi,
and, because the voters were divided,
Congress by the narrowest of margins
gave the presidency to John Q. Adams.
Charles went to Yale where, in his twenties,
he would learn "progressive" ways of thinking.
He read Swift, Rousseau and Carl Linneaus.
Then he studied medicine. His last year,
just before returning to New Orleans,
on a trip to Newport with a classmate
Charles met a whaling captain's daughter.
He proposed. They married and moved south.
Near Old Levee Street on Hospital

Dr. LaRouché opened an office,
stocked it with the latest, most "progressive"
medical equipment, and beside it
moved in with his young wife. Some years later,
after Briseis, their daughter, was born
something overcame the child's mother,
some strange passion no one knew the source of.
In a few months, she was dead, though rumors
spreading through the Creole social circles
claimed she didn't die, in fact, but left home
late one night, stealing aboard a schooner
headed for Barbados or New Zealand.
Some said she was mad and couldn't master
French and Creole manners. Strictly rumors
these were. In the Catholic cemetery
Charles had a sepulchre erected.
I know little else about this woman
since she rarely left her husband's quarters
and she had no friends. The Parish records,
which I've checked, don't even list a first name.
After his loss, Charles didn't travel
as he had so often as a young man,
nor did he meander through the city
other than to visit patients, purchase
medicines, or take his daughter Bressie
to the Opera.

This daughter Bressie,
though suppressing moments of disquiet,
grew up easily. And she was lovely —
I can say this. I would later know her.
Maybe I should wait and not describe her
as a girl but only as a woman.
Bressie had that kind of complex beauty
hidden in an adolescent's gestures
like the tucking in of loose or stray hairs
behind the ears, or the constant tugging
at the bodice girls do when they're nervous,
wondering how their breasts show, I imagine.
(What do I know, though, of being fourteen
and a girl?)

I've seen a portrait of her
painted by the Parisian, Alfred Boisseau,
whom the doctor had commissioned. In it

though she's barely seventeen, already
she has hazel eyes aglow with ardor,
linking intellect with restless passions,
feline eyes, but lacking feline cunning.
Funny but when she and I were lovers,
I was sure her eyes were green. However,
I have learned since then that Monsieur Boisseau
disregarded nature in his portraits,
especially those of his wealthier patrons.
My desire is not to be fantastic,
but to put things as they really happened,
so portraying Bressie's eyes as hazel
or green could mislead you. They were neither
but would change according to the daylight:
hazel in the morning, green at dusk,
almost black at night. It doesn't matter.
In her portrait you can see her shoulders
bared, with one of those white frilly blouses
drawn around her upper arms and bosom.
Monsieur Boisseau paints her skin bright yellow,
as though she has caught tuberculosis
and won't see her twenties; I remember
how her skin would redden in the sunlight
like a black man's. Not that she was that dark.
And she wasn't chinless! Monsieur Boisseau,
following the fashion, gives her no bones;
my guess is she had her mother's features,
her distinctive jawline and her strong mouth,
not her father's genteel Creole roundness.
He contributed the auburn color
of her hair and eyebrows. And her fingers,
which were delicate. And her gentlenesses.
I'll withhold the rest till she undresses.

5

Charles, though he didn't travel, did read —
ethics, politics, the law — and sometimes
he would page through Walter Scott or Shakespeare.
Also, he read *Eugene Aram*, *Typee*,
Clarendon's *History of the Rebellion*,
Belphegor by Machiavelli, Prescott's
Phillip II, Dickens' *Pickwick Papers*,
Motley's *Memoirs of a Young Provincial*,

and *DeBow's Review* and *Harper's Monthly*.
"Slavery," he wrote in '57,
"cannot last another decade. Sadly,
those who don't believe me will pay dearly."
So when Beauregard besieged Fort Sumter,
Charles left New Orleans for New Haven.
Strangely, he had never told his daughter
of his prophecies about secession,
not since Bressie's husband's yellow fever.
Nor did he ask her to go north with him
but departed early one spring morning
on a steamer headed for New Haven,
leaving just a note inside his foyer.
Bressie found it when she came to visit,
two days later, from her house upriver
between Bacchus and Apollo Streets
on Erato, in the Anglo District.
He wrote that he loved her, not to worry,
he'd return, once all of this blew over,
he'd no peace of mind here in New Orleans,
knowing what he knew (*Knows what?* she wondered).
He would wait till things fell into place.

His note frightened Bressie. Sudden changes
always in the past had frightened her —
when, at seven, she had had to disrobe
for a man who called himself her "maître":
It was August but she shivered. His hands,
sweating, held fast to her shoulders. He said,
"*Oui*, but aren't you pretty, little one!"
She was scared that she might catch pneumonia.
After that she told herself she'd never
thoughtlessly undress again. Or later
when she married but could not say why.
Or throughout her husband's illness. *Changes*,
she'd resolved, *demand both eyes stay open*
to the end, as when you dive in water
suddenly, then rise toward the surface.

Planning to seek out an explanation,
Bressie caught an omnibus the next day
down St. Charles to Canal, then crossed there
to the office of the *Daily Crescent*.
Should she leave New Orleans, too, for safety?
Was her father guilty? Would the Parish

confiscate her house? She had no children
(all my sources have agreed on this point)
and was widowed, with no other family
known to her, except her Uncle Bandeaux —
really not her uncle, I learned later,
but her second cousin once removed.
At the office of the *Daily Crescent*,
she was greeted by a man with rolled sleeves
sitting at a printer's table. Rising,
he removed his glasses, then glared at her.

"I have come to hear about this war,"
Bressie said, for lack of something better.

"War?" The man looked stumped, as though the word *war*
had no place in French or English, "What war?"
Rubbing one hand on his bald head, he asked,
"Do you mean that skirmish at Fort Sumter?"

"Yes," she said. Her shoulders drooped. "My father —
he's a doctor — he says we can't triumph,
that our world is changing for the better,
that the future's here. So how am I to —
what should I do? What will happen — ?"

"Madam,"
intervened the man, his nose upturning,
"Stay calm. Nothing's going to happen."

"But, sir. . ."
Bressie didn't take dismissal lightly.
She resisted him. Like other women
with her background, she read few newspapers,
but that didn't mean she wouldn't read them
if she had a reason to. To Bressie,
governments were playthings of the devil,
not the tools of men, as Charles argued.
She imagined laws as exercises
men perform to place themselves in power.
Women, if they please the ghosts inside them,
never need to manufacture power,
just a language to express it, language
men manipulate instead of master.
Power, language, kindness, words of longing,
human beings burning with a fever,

matching kind with kind, belonging, yearning,
words, words disappearing, water, drowning.
Wait! Wait! Focus, Bressie. There is nothing
to survive us. Nothing, Davenport. Still,
focus.

"There will be no war," the man said,
"Louisiana is a sovereign state.
Lincoln can't declare war without admitting
we've become an independent nation.
Independence is our cause *precisely.*
Should *le président* desire war, we will
by his very declaration triumph.
Men may die in skirmishes; already
several have. But there's no cause for worry,
Madam. You're safe. Should you not believe me,
go ask General Lovell at the State House."

Bressie bought the *Crescent* and departed.
Three o'clock. The April sun was blazing
on two soldiers picketing the State House
who watched a woman pass, but on Royal
shadows fell toward the east, where Bressie
under their protection stepped inside
seeking him in whom she might confide.

6

What about this Bandeaux, Bressie's uncle?
Why should she not go to him? He loved her,
surely. Like a father he'd protect her.
But she wasn't looking for protection
nor for words of idle reassurance.
Have I made this evident? No husband,
father nor confederate could know this
since New Orleans has its own traditions,
which both Charles and Bressie's husband heeded.
Bandeaux, on the other hand, was "different."
Slightly hunchbacked, he was barrel-chested
with a long, sharp nose and narrow fingers.
On Dumaine he managed his own art shop
and salon called Studio des Artistes.
Boisseau went there, as did G.D. Coulin,
Marie Adrien Persac, John Genin,

Poincy, Rudolph Lux, Achille Perilli
(painter of dead animals) and others.
Some here still remember Bandeaux fondly,
how he'd flatter them and hang their paintings
up and down his fourteen-foot-high walls.

One night in the fall of 1860
six months after Bressie's husband's funeral,
she succumbed to Bandeaux's constant coaxing
that she let her old friend, Helen Clairborne,
escort her to one of his "art evenings."
There Madeira flowed like the Niagara.
Fruits were piled high in baskets — peaches,
dates, figs, apples, melons, plums — while peanuts,
walnuts, hazel nuts, pecans and almonds
overindulged the whetted appetites of
actors, artists, poets and musicians.
Bressie didn't like these people. They were
careless with their language. But their actions
she could sympathize with — the actress breaking
like a siren into Schubert's lieder,
imitating Jenny Lind's soprano,
painters spitting melon rinds at rivals
or at their own paintings, sending Bandeaux
up his ladder after them, the poet
raising toasts to Sophocles, reciting
choruses from *Oedipus*, then fainting.
No one paid attention to each other
at this mélange, except Bandeaux, who would
snatch a bottle from his servant Crispus,
prop himself atop his stool, and watch them
galavant across the room, his fingers
curled around his glass like tiny serpents
sniffing half-eaten fruit.

"Helen," Bressie asked the morning after,
as they breakfasted in Bressie's courtyard,
"what are they afraid of, all these artists,
that they must destroy themselves?"

"It's beauty,"
Helen answered rather dreamily,
as she gazed up at the bare mimosas
bathed in late October light, "Remember
how the spring rains nourishing those blossoms

turned to thunderstorms, then ravished them,
dropping each poor flower to the ground
so this autumn sun could warm us?"

"Blossoms?
Once I would collect them," answered Bressie,
idly, "I would lay them out and dry them,
then I bound them in a pretty garland —
for my hair, you know, — for beauty's sake."
Was that the wreath she wore into the lake?

7

But no blossoms flowered in her hair
when she went to Lovell for his counsel
after LaRouché's departure. Kindly,
Lovell greeted Bressie, taking both hands,
noting her black widow's dress. They sat.
Facing her, he set his elbows firmly
on his chair's arms, then leaned slightly forward
toward her, shoulders squared, expression steady,
as though he were sitting for a portrait.
She, distracted by his large brass buttons,
had an impulse to reach out and touch them,
feel the heat there emanating from them.
Little fires, she thought. But then her eyes dropped,
as she smoothed the wrinkles in her full skirt,
and she summoned words she thought she needed
to persuade this man that she was faithful
to his cause.

What words she spoke require
no recounting here. What passed between them
passes everyday between men and women,
whether they are intimates or strangers.
It's the commerce of desire: **I want**
this result, and I want you to want it,
too. I'll know then I have been accepted.
But I understand the risk of wanting,
how we die for it, and so I offer,
in return, my vulnerability,
secrets I can't start to share with you here
but expressed in gestures — yes, I trust you.
Lovell offered words of reassurance

yet he didn't make her feel indebted.
Maybe it was his eyes turning downwards
like hers. Maybe he knew Bressie's father
couldn't return, unless thousands died first.
Maybe fires *did* burn in his buttons,
fueled by passions hidden from his eyes.
As he spoke to her intently, Bressie,
leaning toward him, watched his lips in motion
like a priest's in granting absolution.

"Sometimes we receive reports," said Lovell,
"monitoring military business
in the north. I'll ask after your father,
where he may be staying. Please come see me,
if you need assistance or have trouble."
Then he took her hands in his. She thanked him.
True, when certain more distinguished ladies
(Creoles, mostly) learned of Charles's absence,
Bressie was soon banished from their parlors:
They assumed her father was a traitor.
And was she not somehow culpable
for the premature death of her husband?
Besides, rumor had it her own servant,
Alexander, sometimes dined with her!
"Massa Kinsman" Bressie's neighbors called him.
Bressie didn't care about their parties
too much, since she had her own friends (Helen
and two or three younger, unmarried women).
But once word got out that Lovell knew her
and regarded her the "autumn flower
of New Orleans," an epithet he gave her
when one night apparently his senses
overtook his usual composure —
in the company of one of those
cunning women, who cannot be trusted,
who by their proximity and magic,
by the showing of their necks in slanted
light, or with a graceful word, seduce you
into sharing your most cherished secrets —
no one after that, from what I've gathered,
talked to Bressie rudely or abused her,
though I know one tried to.

As for Lovell,
not in public documents nor letters
does he ever mention Bressie's visit.

He fulfilled his promise to her
by attempting to protect her city.
That failed. More than two years later, Bressie,
having lost her home, would hear from Lovell
after his retreat to Brashear City.
Wait. No one controls the future, Bressie,
and no one, Davenport, can know the past.
One makes things up, hoping they will last.

8

The same day Bressie visited the State House
Lovell's younger cousin Brutus Trosler,
First Lieutenant Colonel White, stayed busy.
As her life changed, he was changing others'
by the levee, where the new enlistments,
raw Louisianans from upriver,
signed themselves away. They called him Trosler,
this man standing over six feet tall,
squarely built, though not too large, his black hair
slicked down with pomade, his mustache trimmed
unlike most Confederates who sported
bushy beards and mustaches, his eyebrows
dark, dark eyes below them.

(For the record
I must note here that I only saw him
once myself, I think, that time he watched me
from a bluff across the Mississippi
at Port Hudson. I'm sure it was Trosler
with his loaded musket pointed at me.
Even after forty days of fighting,
cut off from supplies, he somehow managed
to obtain pomade to keep his hair slicked.
We were living on hardtack and coffee,
using ferns for bandages, and sleeping
with acanthuses. But still I knew him,
black hair glistening in the sun, pomaded.)

By the wharves he organized batallions,
lined them up and marched them to Canal Street
for induction. Mostly adolescents,
they'd hitched rides on steamers down the river
from St. Joseph, Ferriday, New Carthage,

or Vidalia, never having traveled
more than twenty miles from their families
or their farms before. But now this rumor
of a war for slavery had brought them,
by the thousands, to New Orleans. Never
had they seen the likes of this strange city;
never would they see her likes again.
Twelve months later I would feel the same way,
though I wouldn't find her in her glory
when the slave exchange was thriving, women
graced the boulevards in summer dresses,
European sailors intermingled
with the whites, Creoles and free men of color
in the bustling streets (those streets now empty
save for these Northeastern opportunists
who have come here looking for positions
in the newly formed state government
or, if not there, in the music parlors).
More than pick the pockets of the wealthy,
these recruits, as Trosler knew, were eager
to encounter everywhere new women,
city women, soft, sophisticated
and erotic in their ruffled panniers,
fine silk blouses curled around their bosoms,
straw hats trailing ribbons, powdered faces
smiling distantly, and white, bared ankles —
or, if not them, their more sensual sisters
lingering in the Vieux Carré, with no skirts
hiding their red petticoats. Saliva
swilled the throats of these young country bumpkins.
Back at home their mamas sternly warned them
how Orleaners stump the devil: Satan,
they said, when he's trading, never bothers
bartering for souls down in New Orleans.
Most Orleaners don't care much to be saved
and, besides, there's little they will trade for
since they have the things they want already —
whisky, loaded dice, sweet whores, and silver,
even thunderboxes lined with silver!

Trosler, though a native of New Orleans,
was taught by his Anglo merchant father
to demand control. An expert horseman
and a model soldier trained at West Point,
he barked orders at these hapless greenhorns

even before they left the wharf: "Attention!
Stand in files with four abreast! Keep shoulders
straight, back straight, head straight, your eyes faced forward.
Quickly! Quickly! This is not a picnic!
You may think you're all about to enter
heaven. Heaven God reserves for angels.
Though you have been well-paid for enlisting
and better paid for signing up your friends,
you have not been brought here to get wealthy,
drink too much and chase your favorite lady.
You are here to save your independence!
To protect your homeland from invasion!
Keep yourself in rank there! And remember
anyone caught drinking to excess
will be brought before a strict tribunal.
Anyone caught gambling will be locked up.
Anyone caught sleeping while on duty
will be executed on the spot.
True, while anyone caught with a woman
cannot be, by military order,
punished for it, still the flesh is weak, men!
Like an untrained stallion. Love's a hollow
women may fall into, but not us.
Forward! I want to see you kick up dust!"

9

Several hundred country boys in burlap,
buckskin jackets, pantaloons, all marching
awkwardly across the Old Town Square,
Trosler shouting at them, "Left! Right! Left! Right!"
as he passed among them with his sword drawn,
pricking this one's three-day beard, or slapping
with his blunt blade that one's thighs or kneecaps,
herding them across the square, then halting
briefly, then returning to Old Levee,
right toward Canal, left to the State House
where they would be given heart and eye tests,
regulation uniforms and blankets,
and, at last, the money they'd been promised
for enlisting. Marching down Old Levee
they passed wagons on the way to market
piled up with vegetables or fresh fruit.
Carriage drivers jerked their horses sideways

toward the gutters, to avoid this strange crew,
this off-season Mardi Gras parade, brash
would-be revelers in homespun breeches
bumbling over brickholes, out of step,
stealing glimpses at the crowd, then tripping
over the legs of those stumbling before them,
dragging their feet and gawking.

B.T. White,
Prince of these Louisiana Knights,
strutted forward, one hand on his scabbard,
one hand brandishing his polished weapon,
out erect, and ready for the charge!
During this procession, like a monarch
he would turn his head from side to side
to attract the wide, admiring eyes
of the women on the banquette, bowing
slightly, with his condescending smile
like the valiant smile Perseus offered
to Andromeda before he dragged her
from Poseidon's rock, a hero's smile.
Sometimes he'd touch his sword to his hat brim,
tip it, turn, and carry on. Poor Trosler.
His clear, bright, pale skin, his trim black mustache,
and his mock brigade at half attention
innocently lumbering behind him.
Some of these would soon become the Zouaves,
Turcos, Chasseurs de Pied, and Tigers.
Some of them would suffer but survive.
Most of them would die. But on that first day
what a spectacle they must have made there
marching proudly to Canal, those raw troops
who would train, then travel north in railcars
to Virginia, Tennessee, Kentucky,
Georgia, Alabama, Mississippi,
Jackson, Johnston, Pemberton, Polk, Mouton,
Beauregard and Lee, before they'd tire
of imagining themselves for glory,
aging twenty years a day. Still, here now,
brave and cavalier, they heard around them
cheers that echoed cheers you may remember
from those epic tales the poets sang of
long ago, to fill your nights of leisure
with King Arthur, Charlemagne, and Caesar.

10

Back to Bressie. It had been a year now
since her husband's death. But still she "mourned" him,
only wearing black clothes out in public.
When at home, though, lingering near her armoire,
she might sift for hours through her old clothes —
hoopskirts, skirts of crinoline, silk blouses,
dresses flounced with lace, long ruffled panniers,
black merino waists, sheer satin sashes,
gowns with puffed, meshed shoulders, cotton nightgowns,
petticoats she'd had imported one spring
after she had read a book on Paris,
summer dresses, winter kirtles, spring gowns
all dyed colors foreign to her now —
pink, green, lavender, maroon, and yellow —
linked to her past. Sometimes she would dress up
like a doll, for fun, to see if these things
fit her still. She'd waltz around her bedroom,
humming Meyerbeer or Mozart. Rarely
would she wear these clothes downstairs, she told me.
She was too embarrassed to. Besides,
often she found Alexander down there
pacing in the hall, or in the library
flipping through a book.
(Shall I imagine
what was passing through that strange man's mind then?
Recently, I heard he's been appointed
to the Louisiana Legislature.
Later. This is not a freedman's story.)

Look up from the page now. Picture Bressie
dancing silently before her mirror,
wearing just a silk chemise or nightgown.
Or, if you're distracted by her image,
maybe you prefer to think your own thoughts,
tired of mine. I can't say I blame you.
Truth is not remotely as exciting
as the authors of most modern books
would have you believe. Please. Take a moment.
Find a mirror. Look at your reflection.
What do you see? Picture Bressie that way.

Late this afternoon before her armoire,
she is searching for a gown, a brown one,

light brown like the color of her hair,
brighter than her other mourning dresses,
pleated, cut with ruffled sleeves, its collar
gathered modestly. This is the first time
since her husband's fever she is going
to the Opera. Since then La Calve,
once the best soprano in the country,
Mr. Boudousquie's wife, has retired.
Helen claims the Opera itself might
soon be closed. "We simply must go see it,"
she's insisted, "Everyone will be there!
Who knows when we'll have another chance, dear,
if this war goes on like this! Besides,
Boudousquie's presenting his discovery,
La Calvé's replacement, just a young girl,
but with a voice sweeter than a siren's!"

Bressie has missed going to the Opera.
She has missed the tonic of its theatre —
melodies of private pain and pleasure
offered to the world, not with dishonor,
but with style: applause, bright costumes, flowers,
gentlemen in tails in family boxes
from which they watch not just the performance
but the women in the loge grillées,
who demurely raise their screens, lean forward,
and arrange themselves to best advantage.
Singing, "*Ombre légère qui suis mes pas*,"
from Dinorah's Shadow Song, while dressing,
Bressie pins her hair with silver hairpins
which, she knows, will sparkle in the gaslight.
Next she lifts a necklace with a pendant,
rose-shaped, from her jewel box, then two brooches,
also rose-shaped. All are polished silver.
She is worried they're too ornamental
for a widow. Still, she likes their texture.
Gently, reaching back to pull her hair up,
she secures the necklace clasp and, turning,
looks at her reflection where her full breasts,
lifted by her corset, cradle the pendant.
Looking down, she cups the rose with one hand,
touching its fine texture with two fingers.
Delicately lined as nature's own rose,
she recalls, her mother said. At one time
both this necklace and the rose-shaped brooches

“Giant Steamboats on the Levee at New Orleans” by Hippolyte Sebron, 1853. Courtesy of Newcomb Art Department of Tulane University.

"Maison Ponchartrain Nouvelle Orleans" by Nicolino Calyo, 1848. Courtesy of Ogden Museum of Southern Art.

were a gift her father gave her mother
on return from Italy. **They're mine now**,
she thinks, wondering what has made her think that.
Then she takes a pair of small pearl earrings,
goes downstairs, and, joining Alexander,
walks with him to Helen's on Euterpe.
There, by the columned promenade stands waiting
Helen's carriage, as the daylight's fading.

11

I admit I've not seen many operas.
These days when I go out to hear music
usually it isn't by Rossini
but those bayou fiddlers who sing French songs
mixed with hoots and howls. Not so for Bressie.
She preferred more subtle strains of music.
Also, while I'm always late, or hurried,
Bressie liked to get to places early,
to absorb the surge and flow of people
gathering, like water to a delta.
On the night I'm trying to imagine
Helen had booked for them a loge grillée.
Once behind their screen, they watched the crowds come
in a perfume-scented buzz, while Helen,
ever feigning transcendental thoughts, mused
over that night's tragedy, *The Masked Ball*,
recently the rage of all New York.

"Verdi knows a woman's spirit," she sighed,
"better than Donizetti or Rossini.
Such devotion! Such divine submission!
I am thinking of Luisa Miller,
of course. Don't you hope — " she started skimming
quickly through her program, " — hope Amelia
will be like Luisa, sweet and passive?"

"What about Lucia de Lammermoor?"
Bressie answered, though she kept her eyes fixed
on three uniformed men who stood chatting
to themselves, beside a nearby baignoire,
"True, Luisa dies from breaking her vows.
Isn't it because her father makes her...,
no, that's wrong. Her father doesn't make her

leave her lover. What's his name?

"Rodolfo?"

Helen offered.

"But that double bass — "

"Würm?" Helen asked, her voice dropped lower
in an imitation of the music.
"VOO-ARM!" she sang, dropping even lower,
"VOO-ARM É PERFIDO."

"Stop, you silly — "

"VOO-ARM É PERFIDO," she repeated,
"What an absolutely horrid monster!"

Bressie watched the three young uniformed men
flit, like three mosquitoes near a tidepool,
toward an open loge, where four young women,
fanning themselves, didn't seem to notice.
"Poor Lucia dies of grief," she added,
"Only minutes separate, by mere chance,
happiness from death, . . . when Edward — "

"*Gar*,"

chided Helen, "*Gar*. Ed-*gar*."

"Ed-*gar*, then —
when he comes too late to stop her marriage
to the wrong man." Bressie glared at Helen.
"Care to tell me his name?"

Helen, pressing
two gloved fingers to her lips, just twinkled.

"Anyway," continued Bressie, "Verdi,
I agree, is good. I never could tell
whether or not Lucia could be happy
married to a man gallant as Edgar,
even had he offered her the chance to."

Alexander lounged behind them. Bressie,
waiting for the concertmaster, chatted
more about Lucia, how young she seemed

truly to know what love is, pain is, loss is.
"I guess that's why she obeys her father
rather than her heart," she said and looked out
through the lattice for the three young soldiers
who, their backs now turned to her, were laughing
with the women in the side loge.

"Goodness!"
Helen blurted, reading from her program,
"This Amelia is married! Gracious!
Are you sure, my dear, that you can face this?"

12

For the inexperienced: Mostly
operas tell the histories of lovers,
those who, due to outside circumstances,
usually are torn apart. *The Masked Ball*,
or, that is, *Un Ballo in Maschera*,
for example, from what I have learned since,
tells the story of a Count Ricardo,
Governor of Boston. He has two foes —
Tom and Sam are their names. Both are black men!
I don't know much, but I've been to Boston
and I've never heard of any count there.
Let it be. Ricardo loves Amelia,
but she's married to his secretary
who is also his best friend, Renato.
Tom and Sam, Renato learns, are planning
to assassinate his boss. Ricardo,
in the meantime, wants to throw a masked ball,
not one of those staid affairs in Boston
but more like a fancy Carnival gala,
which, I'm sure, appealed to all the Creoles
in the theatre. Let it be, Sir Loris.

In the first act, reading from his guest list,
realizing Amelia will be there,
poor Ricardo languishes with passion
for Renato's wife. His pain and anguish
have no equal. Still, he knows he's happy
he will see her soon, and business being
business, he must first endorse a warrant
for the banishment of one, Ulrica,

Negress fortune teller, whom one, Oscar,
Ricardo's slave, pleads for the defense of.
On a whim, the Count decides to go see,
for himself, this sorceress to test her
on the rumors of this plot to kill him.
But when he arrives, he finds Amelia
crying in Ulrica's tent, confessing
her undying love for Count Ricardo!
Quel coincidence! Poor Amelia!
She's betrayed Renato! But Ricardo,
hiding in the fortune teller's closet,
celebrates ecstatically. Ulrica,
meanwhile, bids Amelia go at midnight
off to a forbidden cemetery
where she must pluck some strange mystic herb
which will cure her infidelititis.
Soon Amelia leaves. Ricardo enters
and he asks Ulrica who will kill him.
"Whosoever takes you by the hand next,"
she replies, the moment when Renato,
worried for Ricardo's safety, enters,
grabs his friend's hand warmly, innocently,
and rejoices. Then the chorus joins in,
Tom and Sam included, those *perfidos*.

As the screen descended on this first act,
Bressie restlessly stood up. Requesting
Alexander please to fetch her champagne,
she watched through the lattice, as the crowd cheered
wildly. Helen couldn't stop from cooing,
lovingly repeating every detail
of Amelia's looks, Ricardo's costume.
Bressie couldn't listen to her too long
so she gazed up at the thick white columns
on the stage. From everywhere around her,
from the boxes, from the balconies,
from behind, and from above, whirred whispers
like a Latin chant at Mass that rises
in unbroken unison toward heaven,
every voice intoning, *Adelina!*
Adelina! Adelina!, whispers
reverently ascending, *Adelina!*
soon to fill the place of La Calvé
as the best soprano in the world,
What a dazzling voice! A lovely woman!

Adelina! every voice repeating,
Adelina! Adelina Patti!

Suddenly, the years of quiet living —
learning how to walk with toes faced forward,
how to dress demurely, how to undress
gracefully, how to obey her father,
how to act with kindness toward her husband,
how to soothe his bed sores, how to bathe him
when his fever burned, how to pick flowers,
bind them, make a garland, then a nosegay
for his funeral bower — years descending
over her like clouds of cold air swirling,
sinking from the troisiémes, a cold fog
filled with memories that had escaped her
now engulfing her — her childish yearning
to become a man when she grew up,
how she took a mulecar with her uncle
to Lake Pontchartrain when she was just fourteen,
how she'd taken off her petticoat
to go swimming, unafraid of mudfish,
alligators, or her uncle's scolding,
how the brackish water felt on her skin,
small drops clinging to her forehead, moisture
soaking through her slip, warm surges under
her thighs, where her skirt was gathered, swelling,
swollen waves of darkness passing through her,
through her lips, her throat, her hips, her torso.
She remembered thinking, **Am I drowning?**
Do I want this darkness to swallow me?
Then she almost fainted, Helen chatting
incoherently, while all around her
Adelina! Adelina! whispers
rose, in wave on wave of shadows, upward.

Through the X's crossing on her lattice,
through the shadows, Bressie saw a figure,
probably a man's. By leaning forward,
she could lift the lattice screen, and *whoosh!*
gaslight flooded through the darkness, cool air
rushed in. Bressie started panting, panting,
slumping back into her chair. Mid-sentence,
Helen stopped her chatter. Alexander
from behind walked in with two small glasses
on a silver tray, while there before her

that dark figure Bressie'd seen, its back turned,
whirled around instinctively to face her,
having heard the *whoosh!* behind it. Throwing
her head back, inhaling deeply, Bressie
shut her eyes. She felt the gaslight on them,
burning off those dark waves in a rhythm
mimicking her heartbeat. With her eyes closed
all she saw was red. But that dark figure,
she sensed, was approaching, like a shadow
dampening the fire behind her eyelids.
She looked up and found a well-dressed soldier
staring at her, as at some rare painting
on a wall at Bandeaux's art shop.

"Bressie!
Darling!" Helen laughed to break the tension,
"Why, I do believe you've scared this colonel
half to death! You poor soul! Have some champagne."

Bressie couldn't tell whom Helen meant,
she herself or this dark, speechless colonel,
so she raised a gloved hand to her moist lips,
brushed them with her fingertips, and squeaked
like a baby sparrow. She smiled faintly.

Just as meagerly the colonel smiled.

"I was startled. By the noise," he told her,
bowing at the neck.

"Though not, I trust, sir,"
Helen interjected, "as much as by
Adelina's hypnotizing aria?"

"Uh," the colonel mumbled, "it was charming."

Pause.

He glanced at Bressie, who was sipping
from her glass, as she felt fresh blood coursing
through her veins again.

Brring! Brring!

"Excuse me,"

begged the man. His face dropped like a dead branch.
"There. The bell. The second act. Excuse me."
Blushing pink, he rushed back to his baignoire.

In the second act, the good Renato,
to protect Ricardo from the killers,
sticks by him as they traipse through the forest
where, behold! they run into Amelia.
But Renato doesn't recognize her
since she, cleverly, has put a veil on
in the guise of a religious woman.
Smart Ricardo doesn't breathe a word.
But Renato, who fears Sam and Tom
coming at the Count from every corner,
urges his friend to go home alone
by a secret pathway only he knows.
Ricardo won't! Not unless Renato,
promising that he won't speak with her,
takes this woman back with him. Renato,
never questioning his boss's motives,
swears an oath. Ricardo makes his exit.
Yet before the other two can make it
through the darkness safely back to Boston,
Tom and Sam surprise them on the highway!

But, since they're just looking for Ricardo,
Tom and Sam decide to spare this couple,
choosing only to strip the woman's veil off
and discover whom the Count's been courting:
It's Amelia!

Here the crowd starts swooning,
usually. Bressie was no exception.
Shocked Renato breaks into hysterics,
giving his wife no chance to explain things.
Melodies of private pain and passion
follow. Then Renato sings a solo
which explains why he must kill Ricardo,
his best friend, for having so betrayed him.
Then the second intermission.

Trosler,
though he longed to do so, didn't visit
Helen's loge, its lattice now wide open.
She who'd raised it, when the houselights went up,

didn't seem to notice he was watching.
How does Adelina keep her throat wet?
Trosler wondered, as he felt his own throat
cracking from the gas. He shut his eyes,
tensing with his own heart, then relaxing
as the pounding in his veins subsided.
Rising, he crossed to a group of soldiers
but positioned himself at an angle
where he might observe the woman he'd seen
sitting with her friend, who now was weeping
over Adelina's fate. He eyed them
but restrained himself from going back there
since, though he looked calm enough, his blood was rushing
and he'd not disgrace himself again by blushing.

13

What a shock for Trosler to be taken
for a fool! He couldn't shut his eyes
without seeing her there, head thrown backwards,
panting, panting, almost like a racehorse
at a steeplechase before the arm falls,
restless, anxious to be in the open,
eyes half-closed, as though the world were too much
to be taken in a single glance,
silver brooches sparkling. And that curve there
at the base of her neck, where her shoulders
hold her breasts. **She must be Creole**, he thought,
What had her friend called her? Bessie? Trishy?
He must learn about her. **Is she married?**
He had not looked at her hands. **Who is she?**
He had never seen a woman like her.

Soon he started thinking of the battles
he still had to fight. In less than three weeks
he was supposed to take his troops to Jackson,
there to ride a train to Memphis, Richmond,
and beyond that, north to Shenandoah.
Until this evening, Trosler'd wanted nothing
other than to prove himself in battle.
Each day, drilling men at the Metairie,
he would proudly ride among them, boasting
not about his expert horsemanship,
nor about what he would do to Yankees

whose misfortune it might be to meet him
as they made their arbitrary way
through some field, on which he'd decimate them,
sending what was left of them to Heaven
where a greater judge than he would judge them
for their untoward miscalculation
which had brought them face to face with Trosler
in the first place. No. Instead, he boasted
of the First Louisiana's horsemen.
Thanks to them, the nation's independence
was secure forever. Thanks to them
God's commandments would prevail!

This woman,
he thought, **what is she but some diversion,**
probably the music, my impatience,
her disturbing gesture when I saw her
with her screen raised. Must stop thinking of her.
Then he wondered if she had a lover.

14

We are older, but we're none the wiser
having suffered five years with a war on.
Yesterday while walking down Dumaine Street
near where Bandeaux used to have his art shop,
I was startled by a man who almost
knocked me over.

"Sir!" I cried, impassioned.
Stumbling past me, he said nothing. **Drunkard**,
I thought to myself, as off he wandered
toward the river. Rubbing up against me,
he'd knocked some substance from his wrinkled jacket
onto mine. I brushed it off, then noticed
it was neither dirt nor dust but sea salt.
During the war, hard salt was expensive,
unaffordable. Black marketeers
smuggled huge sacks of it across the lake
where for twenty times the going prices
they would sell it by the pound, or trade it
for munitions, seegars, or good whisky.
Further up Dumaine I saw a woman
standing with her one fist cocked at her waist

and the other holding up a broomstick.
Salt was sprinkled all across the banquette
like an onion snow in Pennsylvania.
Glaring past me at the stumbling black man
as he disappeared, she was tapping
with her broomstick on the banquette: Hoodoo.
She was ridding herself of a freedman.
I realized he had no whisky in him,
only fear. The salt she'd sprinkled on him
had condemned him to ten years of bad luck,
while the broom, when waved across his body,
doomed him to an early grave. The poor man
shouldn't have tried asking her for money;
I shouldn't have assumed he was a black man
just like any other; her mistake was
playing carelessly with others' magic.
Too soon careless actions will turn tragic.

15

But where was I? O, yes. Trosler's illness.
Bandeaux tended to his friends and neighbors
as a beekeeper to his bees. Their honey
he collected for himself, but never
did he let one sting him. Spotting Trosler
staring dumbly at an oil painting
at his shop one day, he sensed that something
extraordinary was afoot here.
He was propped atop his stool, as usual,
from where he might watch the daily traffic,
but this handsome soldier was so pale,
any minute now he might vanish.
True, his black hair was pomaded neatly
but a long slick hung across his forehead
down between his bloodshot eyes. His jacket
on one sleeve was mud-stained, his inside collar
sweaty, and his buttons not all buttoned.
To his side, his scabbard dangled oddly
like a monkey's tail. His boots weren't polished.

The landscape he was gazing at, by Persac,
showed a view of an idealized plantation
on the Mississippi, with its live-oaks,
slaves at work in canefields, powdered ladies,

gracing well-kept lawns and porches, horses
frolicking in fenced-in yards, small children.
Everything around the house was painted
in bright colors — pinks, reds, greens and yellows —
but the vegetation in the forests
and the fields was dark blue, gray, or brown,
so the centerpiece appeared like heaven
circumscribed, or paradise in hell.
Not that any of this bothered Trosler,
blind to all this imagery and haunted
by his rash of recent nightmares. "Fever,"
they had written in his sick-leave letter,
"possibly another epidemic."
Why he'd come here to forget his nightmares
seemed a mystery.

Though it was pleasing,
Bandeaux found the Persac rather trite.
It was odd the way this colonel stared so
at those powdered ladies. What did he want?
Had he met this man somewhere before this?
No. He couldn't place him. "*Pardon moi,* sir,"
Bandeaux whispered, "Do you find that . . . tasteful?"

Trosler balked, as though he'd been awakened
from one of his nightmares. Then he reeled back.
(Am I being obvious? Forgive me.
I am trying to be fair to Trosler
but it's easier to generalize him
as a victim of the times he lived in.
Men must learn to trust each other.)

Bandeaux,
climbing off his stool, said, "Don't you like it?"

"I'm in no position," mumbled Trosler,
"to invest in it. Sorry." Embarrassed,
he brushed back the hair slick on his forehead.

"Not to worry," Bandeaux grinned, "It's pretty."

"I've been ill. As soon as I am better,
I will leave for Richmond," Trosler blurted.

"Richmond?"

"Yes. And, well. Before I go I —
well, a few things ought to, well, be settled.
That is why. I mean, I have good reason —
you might tell me — "

"Would you like a brandy?"
Bandeaux asked.

"Why, yes. Sir. Thank you. Kindly."

Bandeaux hurried Trosler to a chaise lounge
in one corner, through his rear door quickly
disappeared, and in a flash popped back in
with two glasses and a brandy bottle.
"There now, Colonel. I know what the fever
can be like. I lost an in-law to it
not more than a year ago. It's dreadful!"

Trosler sat, recovering from swaying.
"I'm all right," he said, "Your brandy helps, though.
But this dizziness. It handicaps me.
I used to believe that I was destined
for the glory of Louisiana.
Lately, I've been thinking of resigning."

"Colonel! Really! I am flabbergasted!
That a virile man like you would consider
such an act of cowardice." But Bandeaux
wasn't so surprised as he let on.
What he said is what he thought he should say.

"Not from cowardice," responded Trosler,
firmly now, "I'm not equipped to lead them,
my own cavalry. I've lost my spirit.
Vigilance. I'm not afraid of dying.
But what kind of leader is a sick man?"

"Colonel! Suddenly it comes to me!
Yes! You're T.B. White! Now I remember!"
Bandeaux jumped up from the chair he sat in.
"Dr. Palmer's sermon! Lafayette Square!
Last Thanksgiving! You inspired that rally
afterwards. O my, what an occasion!
All the Creoles came out. You were stirring!
Truly. You had everyone there ready —

women, children, even slaves! — to march off
then and there! To go to war! To suffer!"

Trosler smiled as he had at Bressie.

"Yes, of course," sighed Bandeaux, slipping
back into his chair, his shoulders hunched,
as he bit the small tip of one finger,
"You're the model Southron, Colonel. Ah, sir,
I am far too old to go to war
myself. Otherwise I'd join you. Really."
Then he giggled, tilting his head slightly
to the left, then flapping all the fingers
of his right hand through the air beside him.
"*La guerre et l'amour sont pour les jeunes gens*,
as the French say. But now I remember.
You're the one they talk about."

Encouraged,
Trosler stood and, lifting one hand upward,
pressed it flat against his broad lapel,
as though to make sure he was the same man
this man recognized. He touched his buttons,
dangling loose, then buttoned one.

"It's B.T.,
not T.B.," he said, "and here's my question.
I have reason to suspect a lady,
your acquaintance, is a customer here.
She is comely, dark, aristocratic,
and she has a kind of natural grace
that, compared to her, most queens are wretches.
She's a work of heaven, not of fortune."

"Many women come here," Bandeaux answered,
"who no doubt fit that description. I'd say
you are speaking like a man in love.
Mind you, this is just an observation.
Can you be specific, sir?" He eyed him.
"Tell me her proportions. Is, as some say,
those who might write novels on the subject,
is she 'well-endowed with gentle figure'?"

"Well. Yes. Quite," said Trosler. Then he blurted,
"Sir, I think you're joking with me. She is —

though I do admit this woman's pretty —
she is not one I would fall in love with.
She is — "

Pause.

" — a widow. I think. Older.
But not too much older. If she's lonely,
I thought I might call on her. To find out . . .
who her husband was. Or what great struggle
for whose independence he was killed in."
Trosler hurried through this final statement.

"Ah, of course, of course," said Bandeaux, grinning,
"You think *he* might *re*-inspire *you. Oui? Oui?*"

"Yes. That's it."

"A widow? Hmm," thought Bandeaux,
rubbing his chin, "Why do you think I know?"

Trosler turned so red his illness vanished.
"One day I was walking through this district.
Had to get some air. You know. Out walking
to escape the awful suffocation
of my quarters. Doctor said it's healthy.
I was walking by here and I saw her."

"Weren't you quarantined then?" Bandeaux asked him.

"No. Erph. They said I was not suspected
as a carrier." The lips on Bandeaux
rounded in an "O" but no sound came out.

"I had met her at the Opera House.
No one ever introduced us. Well, not
properly. But we exchanged a few words.
Later it was here I saw her. With you.
She wore black clothes. And she had a veil on?
Not more than a week ago. Or ten days."

"You must mean my cousin Bressie! Good Lord!
Why did you not say so in the first place?"
Bandeaux sprang up from the chair he sat in
once again. He rustled through some drawings

stacked together near the wall. "Is this she?"
He extracted Boisseau's painting. "Look! Look!
She is somewhat older now, but look there.
You can tell her by her deep eyes."

"That's her!
What's her name? I need to know."

"It's Bressie,
Bressie LaRouché. Last name's her father's,
not her husband's. We have always known her
as her father's daughter. She's a good girl
but she's not a soldier's widow. He died
from the fever. I already told you."
Then he quickly added, "You're like him, sir . . .
oops!" He clucked. Then lifting up his left hand,
he held back a giggle. "Not that *you* died,"
and a titter leaked between his fingers.
Trosler blushed again, though not as deeply
as before. "This calls for a celebration!"
Bandeaux interjected, "Have a seegar!"
And he pulled out two of his best Cubans,
lighting Trosler's.

"Cousin Bressie's lovely,"
he then reminisced, "You see, I know her
intimately," and he pressed his fingers
in his cheeks and lips, as Trosler purpled.

"O?" said Trosler. He seemed disappointed.
"I mistakenly suspected someone
other. I thought I might know her husband,
that she'd need the solace of another . . . "

"Of another hero? Someone like you?"

"No. I'm not a hero," Trosler answered,
"Not, at least, until I prove myself one."
Then he started dusting off his jacket.

"Nonsense," Bandeaux spoke up, now emboldened,
"Even should you never leave New Orleans,
kill a man, nor fire a musket, Colonel,
after what you did Thanksgiving morning,
leading that parade from Lafayette Square

by Canal Street to St. Louis Cathedral,
you will always be remembered here
as *l'Americain Blanc*. Why, believe me,
General Beauregard gained more supporters
from that one procession through this district
than he can expect again, forever!
We *adore* Napoleonic style,
we Creoles, and we simply crave parades!"
Seeing Trosler's face take on more color,
Bandeaux further flattered him with stories
(some half-false, but most of them half-true)
of how when Governor Moore declared secession
Creoles, with the name *l'Américain Blanc*
ringing in their ears, flocked to enlist.
Next to Beauregard and Mansfield Lovell
they respected more, had more esteem for,
and were more in awe of no one other
than this very man who graced his chambers.
Would he take more brandy? O, the neighbors,
Bandeaux intimated, must have seen him
entering his studio. To please them
he ought really to invite them over.
How they'd *love* to meet the famous Colonel!
But he would defer to Trosler's wishes
for his privacy.

"It's such an honor,"
Bandeaux told him, "having you come visit.
My sweet cousin's often spoken of you.
If she only knew of your concern
and your *special* interest." Then, winking,
he drew closer to his guest and touched him.

Trosler wondered how his sleeve had gotten
mudstained. He felt his sweat soak through his shirt
underneath his jacket. This man's stories,
though he tried denying them, had stirred him.
Yes, how ardently he had paraded
down St. Charles, after Palmer's sermon.
He'd paraded scores of times since then.
But to think that Bressie — what a strange name! —
was there, watching. He'd never be the same.

16

Later when he'd leave the art shop, Trosler,
like that man yesterday I tripped over,
would walk in a daze from some strange malady.
Not the one he came there with, another,
more consuming illness would besiege him:
Optimism.

Bandeaux had assured him
he would tell his cousin of their meeting.
"I am certain, Colonel White," he proffered,
"she will thank me for it."

"Call me Trosler."

"I am honored!" Bandeaux grinned, "And further,
Colonel Trosler, may I have the pleasure
of inviting you to meet my cousin
(at, of course, the proper time and setting)
so you might express to her your feelings?"

"I don't. No. That isn't necessary,"
Trosler said.

"Not necessary? Please, friend,
maybe not for you. But for my cousin?
When she learns she's missed the chance to meet you,
in these trying times, her time of . . . grieving,
who's to say how she might take it? Listen."
Bandeaux reached out, taking Trosler's shoulders.
"Just let me arrange the proper locale.
I am skilled at such things. Don't be modest."
Then he winked. "What good is your concern,
if you never demonstrate it. Maybe
when you're older and you ponder
all the hours you've spent alone, you'll think back
on those feelings never acted on
and you'll praise your moderation. Maybe.
Maybe you'll be proud of never doing
anything — unless, of course to honor
state or family. But what if you don't, sir?
What if, like the artist on his deathbed
who thought only of those masterpieces
he intended painting as a young man

but avoided, for lack of courage, you,
too, should never learn what you are made of?
Maybe you will die happy. But maybe
you must rally to ambition's fanfare,
not just hum along or plug your ears up,
fearful you might lose your self-possession
to her song. The world respects the brave man
who risks life for glory, love, and beauty.
I would think you'd think it was your duty."

17

Trosler gave no answer. He stood, silent,
stunned and elevated by this offer.

"Maybe I'm wrong, but if I know Bressie,"
Bandeaux mused, "she'd love to meet you. Trust me.
I'll take care of all the minor details
and arrangements, if that won't offend you;
you have weightier matters to attend to."

18

Gazing still at Bandeaux in a stupor,
Trosler started to sway. Then he perked up.
"Right!" he barked, "A curse on Lincoln's army!
God protect the brave men of the Southland!"
He took two steps from the chair he'd sat in
and saluted. "God see us through battle!
God lead us to victory!"
Abruptly,
he collapsed, spitting out his seegar
as his brandy glass crashed to the floorboards.
Falling in a faint, he reached for Bandeaux
by the thighs and slid down to his knees.

"Colonel! What are you — are you, you dying?"
Bandeaux bent and hooked his two thin forearms
under Trosler's shoulders, lifting him slowly
to his feet.

"I'm fine. I'm fine," said Trosler,
as a cough that gurgled like a dog's yelp

surfaced from his throat, "A little weakened,
maybe. It's the fever" — cough — "As I was" —
cough — "about to say" — cough, cough — "with God's help" —

Bandeaux, standing breast to breast with Trosler,
felt his hot, smoky breath on his cheekbone —

"we will whip" — cough — "whip" — cough — "them," he added.

"Doubtless, doubtless, doubtless," Bandeaux whispered.

Trosler cleared his throat. "I should be going.
I understand we'll be going north soon,
but I don't expect to be gone too long.
Please commend me to your cousin. Tell her . . . ,
what you will. As long as you are truthful.
And forgive me for this mess I've made here
on your floor."

"It's nothing, nothing, nothing,"
Bandeaux answered.

After they had parted,
Trosler wandered down toward the levee,
as I've told you, in a daze, while Bandeaux
quickly scattered salt across his floorboards.
He was used to cleaning after parties.
As he watched the salt take on the color
of the spilled liqueur, his mind flew elsewhere.
Like an architect who looks at spaces
where there's nothing built but who imagines
marble columns, palaces and temples,
Bandeaux fashioned what he'd say to Bressie,
what her first response might be, his answer,
and the circumstance of their first meeting.

Meanwhile, one who passed him on the street
would think Trosler drunk. But he was radiant,
charged anew with patriotic fervor
yet afraid of dying for the first time
in his life. **He's right. It's necessary
that I reassure this woman**, he thought.
No one recognized him on Old Levee,
as *l'Americain Blanc* followed those steps,
only in reverse, he'd marched so proudly

through the cool breeze that Thanksgiving morning.
Now it was late June. His sweat was soaking
through his shirt. Yet he could feel his fever
dissipating, as though he were waking
from one of those nightmares where the pressure
weighing vaguely on your body slowly
stirs your blood, as you become more conscious,
opening your eyes to a new morning
and you start to celebrate the pleasure,
once again, of living without pain.
He saw in his mind that woman's image
with her parted lips, her eyes closed, panting,
panting, head thrown back, her neck exposed.
Then he pressed his palm on his own forehead,
wiped the sweat away, and felt his skin cooling.

Two days later he went off to Richmond
where he joined with Stuart's cavalry.
Let it be. I won't elaborate on
how he proved himself a model rider
at Manassas, how his reputation
spread as quickly as his pride diminished,
how he lead a charge against the Union
some said was the charge that sent them fleeing
to the woods in disarray, nor later
how he stood with Polk in Tennessee
when they took Columbus in September.
He was wounded there — only a flesh wound.
Somehow he escaped the early traumas
of the war, though often he came close,
and like one who lives near a volcano,
he lay waiting for the next eruption.
There's no pain in waiting, and there's pleasure
knowing someone else will make things happen.
Either you'll be spared or you'll be taken:
Bandeaux found his heart and drove the stake in.

DAVENPORT'S VERSION

BOOK II

1

Why should I go on? There is no reason.
Trosler's almost legend. Bressie's missing.
I'm retained, though mainly as custodian
for the Bureau — which we're closing next year.
I'll return north then to Pennsylvania,
try to find a job there, teaching maybe,
or in a bank. What a fantasy this!
No more a "history" than any life is,
any grasping after scraps of letters,
common smells, the voices one remembers
fading, fading to small whispers, fading
like those bootprints downstairs in the hallway
I tracked in last night. My zealous landlord,
if he ever comes around, will charge me
to remove them; I'm the only Yank here.
By tomorrow morning they'll be vague, though,
harder to identify.

What changes
changes, so that after each mutation
few imagine how they live the same way
others have before them. For example,
how could Trosler spend four months in transit
clinging to that glimpse he'd had of Bressie
in her loge grillée, her eyes closed, panting?
I would have forgotten her in two weeks!
Sooner, if in battle I'd been wounded,
as Trosler was — or as I was, later.
But let me not judge poor Trosler. Surely,
you who chance to read this will accept him,
even if he seems at times outlandish.
Bressie, too, may strike you as peculiar
and the world she lived in now seem foreign.
She grew up before the war, remember.
Still, to me what matters is what matters,
so I mean to show what matters to you
simply, and without excessive comment,
to be straight, uncluttered, calm in feeling,

not so complicated as to lose you.
Even should this poem not amuse you,
may you still see things the way I choose to.

2

But what I write of here, for good reason,
I'm not sure of, though I have a notion
how it must have happened this way:

Bandeaux,
after Trosler set out for Manassas,
slowly set his new plan into motion.
Early one June morning — I say "early"
for a man who often slept past noon,
let's say, ten o'clock — he left his art shop
to return a pair of earrings someone,
some rich temptress from the Anglo District,
had the night before left on his table
after one of his soirees. Why she left them,
why she even took them off, escapes me.
No doubt trying to seduce . . . but whom?
Certainly not Bandeaux! I am lost now:
Women and their jewelry. How they use it
to confuse, to cover, to uncover
what they want a man to know about them.
Often, in the midst of conversation
as I'm on the verge of understanding
something wonderful, some woman stops me,
mumbling, "Sorry. Must remove these bracelets,"
or, "Don't look! I must take off this necklace.
It's too heavy. Painful." Once that's over
and I've lost my line of thought, distracted
by her naked ears, arms, neck, she's talking
off on quite another subject. I'm too,
I admit it, easily distracted,
like a river when it meets an eddy,
spinning off, meandering . . .

So! Bandeaux —
what was I about to say? That Bandeaux,
after visiting this earring woman,
strolled down Nayades over to Erato
where he chanced to call on Bressie, duly

following his family obligation.
She was outside, sitting in her courtyard
with two other women, somewhat younger,
draped on chairs like spring snow on the Piedmont,
their white dresses wilting in the heat.
Tarba, I believe, was one, the other
Antoinette, or Toinette, who said nothing.
They were reading from a book, in German,
each in turn, then whispering, then laughing
nonchalantly, quietly. To Bandeaux
they looked bored. This heartened him, so briskly
down the alleyway he flitted, calling,
"Bressie! Darling! Am I interrupting?"

"Uncle!" she replied obediently,
as she rose and smiled, "You're always welcome."

"I was in the neighborhood. *Bonjour,* girls.
I've been worried, Bressie. I have missed you.
You're not ill, I hope."

"Of course not, Uncle."
Bressie smoothed her dress out with her left hand,
taking Bandeaux's walking stick with her right.
"Please. Sit down with us and have a coffee.
We're reciting Goethe. I should tell you
I'm surprised to see you, but I'm not.
I dreamt of you three times last night."

"Really?
Lovely!" Bandeaux paused to sigh, then plopped down
on the stone bench under the mimosas.
"So you're reading Goethe. What a comfort
during these hard times, these trying times,
when one can't be sure of one's survival."

Bressie's friends exchanged impassive glances.
Then, like herons rising over water
to evade the waves' jetspray, together
they arose and glided from the garden
into Bressie's house, while Bandeaux droned on:
"Such dismay to be without your father,
left alone, defenseless, my dear child,"
and he brought his fingers to his cheek,
brushing them across his lips, "Don't worry.

You have family you can depend on."
Bressie neither frowned nor smiled, her hazel
eyes revealing nothing, waiting for him —
just what does he want?

"Continue reading,
mon chèri. Sit next to me," he beckoned.
She picked up the book and flipped the pages
randomly, until she found a poem.
In a soft voice steady as a banker's
counting out the day's deposits, slowly
she recited:
"*Sagt es neimand, nur den
Wiesen,/ Weil die Menge gleich verhöhnet:
Das Lebendge will ich preisen,/ Das nach
Flammentod sich sehnet. . . .*"

Once she finished,
"Lovely, lovely, sweet," repeated Bandeaux,
"but, alas, it's German. Ich no sprache."

"It's about a butterfly who's darting
straight into a candle flame. In these lines,
'*Und dich reisset neu Verlangen/ Auf zu
höherer Begattung,*' he is praising
flying into fire as a deeper,
more courageous 'union' than to stay hid
in the shade — *'der Finsternis Beschattung.'*"

"Flying into fire as courageous?
Goodness gracious," Bandeaux cried, "How could he?
Sounds like suicide to me. How morbid!
Why would anyone want out of the shade
in such beastly heat as we've been having?"
And he fanned himself. "But tell me, tell me —
let's forget the poetry for now, dear — "
grabbing Bressie's book from her, he slipped it
under his thigh. "Tell me, how have *you* been?"
Yet before she had a chance to answer,
he had changed the subject from her welfare
to the things that interested him — his art shop,
vicious gossip, rumors of the blockade
in the delta, soirees he had gone to.
"Really, *chèri,*" he said, "you should join us.
We have such good times." He raised his right hand,

batting at the humid air beside him,
"I would love to see you dance again.
Why be so unsocial?"

"Lord protect me!
Are you mad?" asked Bressie, "See me dancing?
I'm afraid my dancing days have passed me,
and besides, I'm not exactly wanted
at your soirees, given Father's absence."
Thinking then of Lovell, she inquired
how her uncle thought the "war" was faring.

"War? Why, lovely, lovely, fine. I'll tell you,
in fact, a thing to make you glad the war came,
something that undoubtedly will give you
twenty-five good reasons to start dancing."

"Do you mean the Yankees have conceded?"

"No, not that. But something even better."
Bandeaux seized his chance here.

"Something better?
Come on. Tell me what it is," she urged him,
"since I'm both afraid of what you'll tell me
and excited in anticipation."

Not that she was innocent, exactly.
I remember *our* first conversation
on the train, and how she looked at me then
with her green eyes, as I talked of marching
hour after horrid hour westward
through those canefields she and I were crossing
on our journey eastward to New Orleans.
Listening intently like a child
to a bedtime story, she was silent,
rocking with the click-clack of the traincar
and the rattle of our seats. Embarrassed
by her steady gaze, I dropped my own eyes
to her feet. I felt my blood surge upward
through my legs and arms. Did she believe me?
Was her unassuming look a decoy?

Another time I asked her about talking.
"You like talking," she said, "more than I do."

We had just made love but I was aching
to take her again, to press her body,
feel her breasts against me.

"You don't mean that.
Talk is all we have to know each other."

"Then I guess we don't have much," she answered.

"Don't have much? Then tell me, what else is there?
All I know is that I long to know you."
Turning on my side, I faced her. "Listen,
Bressie." As I touched her with my free arm,
I kept talking. She did not resist me
any more than she had on that train.
She kept calm and didn't interrupt me,
waiting for my words to snare themselves
like loose timber drifting down a river
catching hold in clusters to embankments.

Was that how she listened that June morning
to her uncle, as articulately
with a river pilot's expertise
he avoided all bluffs and abuttals?
First he asked her what she thought of Yankees.
"I don't know," she sighed, "They're like my father,
I suppose. A good man, . . . impercipient
sometimes, . . . but his heart is filled with valor."

"Yes, yes, filled with valor," Bandeaux doted,
"noble, worthy, dignified, et cetera."

"True, some say a Northerner will kill you,"
Bressie added, "just for disagreeing
on a point of law. That's not my father.
He's a Creole, after all, and loves peace."

"What about Confederates, then?" asked Bandeaux,
"Bronze-skinned, fair-eyed, muscular young Southrons?
Don't you think Aeneas would have been proud
to have sailed with such men up the Tiber?"

"Mansfield Lovell is the best example
of that. Everyone has said so."

"*Oui, oui.*
Lovell is well-liked. Yet there's another,
one they mention when they mention Lovell,
one who's second only to his cousin,
one who's risen, though he's not yet thirty
and still has a lovely youthful charm,
to become the Anglos' gem, a colonel,
Colonel B.T. White. And did you know, dear,
he's a friend of mine?"
She pictured Lovell.
Was his manner aged? Or had she been
impercipient, too? "He's Lovell's cousin?"

"*Oui, oui!* One so dauntless as a horseman
Northerners have dubbed him 'The Ghost Raider.'
In a skirmish they would rather die first
at the mercy of some Georgia Cracker
than to face him. He's *l'Américain Blanc*,
do you not remember? A modern hero!
Quite the ideal subject for a portrait.
And what's as important, he's not married."

"Uncle," she protested, "I'm a widow."

"Oh, it's not that I'm suggesting you would . . .,
though, like Guinevere and Lancelot,
you and he . . . . But no, you're right, dear. Only,
not more than a week ago, I saw him —
just before he left — and he was gushing . . .,
gushing over you."

"He what? Some colonel
gushing over me?" Bressie felt naked
in her house dress, missing her black garments.
"Uncle Bandeaux . . . — "
but she drew up silent.
My guess is that, more than Bandeaux's daring,
her formality kept her from talking.
What she felt then, whether she felt yearning,
felt ashamed, or wished to go on reading,
I can't say. But courtesy controlled her:
"Would you like another cup of coffee?"

Bandeaux knew he'd gained the victory, knew
she had not the strength to push him back now.

Like a rose, she'd yielded him her pollen
and her eyes began to water. Blithely,
he handed her his cup. He rose and stretched,
yawning, as she stepped across the courtyard
to the table where the coffee tray was.

"*Finderneice*?" he asked, "Is that the right word?"

"What word?"

"You know. Goethe's word for *shadow*?"
Then he wiped his sweating brow. "This weather,"
he sighed, "What have we done to deserve this?"

She returned and, handing him a full cup,
smoothed her dress where it was clinging to her,
clinging to the contours of her thighs
where the sun had warmed them. Then she looked up
through the trees toward the sky.

"Well, darling,"
Bandeaux said, caressing Bressie's long hair,
"mustn't stay out in the sun forever.
Let's inside. What must your friends be up to?
I'll bet they're just dying to interrupt you."

3

Solitude no one experiences
other than one's own. So, for example,
you might tell me you've been thinking of me
and that bathes my heart — to know I'm thought of
when I'm absent — like a summer shower
coming to alleviate a dry day,
clouds gathering in my imagination.
But if I try picturing you, sitting
at your desk alone, dreaming, or flying
out the door to market, or at midnight
lying in your bed, awaiting sleep,
nothing's there. I simply can't imagine,
when I, like a child who thinks he's magic,
close my eyes and try to disappear,
what it's like for you when you're alone:
I am intimate with *my* detachment

only — which I have presumed is like yours,
for convenience's sake. The rest is fiction.
Solitude, like death, is always other
or one's own. No aura flows within it
to gush forth in waves upon another
who wishes, when he can't, to be drowned in it.

4

During those slow summer days, when Bandeaux
(who had reason now to pester Bressie
and remind her of her "situation")
dropped by every other day, she spent time
by herself, upstairs or in her garden.
Studying both botany and German,
she kept at her reading. Yet her thoughts strayed,
drifting through the mornings, taking no shape
through long afternoons, the heat still rising.
Then, as though awaking from a deep sleep,
suddenly at four or five she'd burst out,
feverishly poring over Schiller
or composing letters to some unknown
or imagined correspondent. Nothing
from those spurts of energy remains now.
Nothing — save one letter sent to Helen
who was spending two months on Grand Isle.
In it Bressie writes about her studies
and her plans to teach orphans that autumn:

> . . . still can't meet expenses, so I've cut back.
> Meat is scarce. I've fish and bread aplenty.
> Chickens, too! But with the money shortage
> things won't be the same this fall. I'm sorry,
> I can't find the flour for those sweetcakes
> you love so. But maybe when I'm teaching,
> though it won't pay much, things will get better.

Later she describes a dream:

> An eagle,
> white as bone, swooped down while I was sleeping
> and attacked me, his extended talons
> ripping out my heart. Then he replaced it
> with his own heart, stealing mine away.

Funny, but I felt no pain nor terror.
What does it mean, one heart for another?
I am thinking of you, Helen.

BRESSIE

What went through her mind? Did she want Trosler,
even though she hadn't met him? Doubtful.
Something tells me she was more inclined then
(I'm as good a source as any here
so indulge me) to meander freely
through her passions, unconcerned with Trosler.
Fine, she'd think, **if this graycoat should want me.**
Let a hundred others follow after,
each the same yet somehow different.
What's a woman that she is so precious
she should be locked up like a deposit
hidden in a vault, like some gold heirloom.
(I imagine her here in her garden,
resting her hip against an oak.) **Really!**
What makes us so mighty? Animals aren't
but their flesh, their muscle, . . . their desire.
Love is just a weak excuse for lying,
making beds more comfortable, . . . for buying
time to make our selfishness unselfish,
to fend off our vicious tendency
to debase each other into seeming
more than animals. We lack the courage
to be animals.
(A sudden shiver,
even though it's now mid-afternoon,
sweeps across her body. Then she grows warm.)

Was she lonely? Did she think of dying
never having tasted her desires?
I confess: Her thoughts are not my own.
Let's move on and leave her thoughts alone.

5

News from Bull Run came. And some weeks later
Trosler, slightly wounded in Kentucky,
was assigned back to New Orleans. First thing,
once he learned the news, sly Bandeaux rushed out

to reset his trap for Bressie.

By now
Mansfield Lovell had been named commander
of all troops in south Louisiana.
He required Trosler's aid to train them.
Frankly, though his cousin's wound was minor,
it provided just the grounds he needed
to bring him back home. Like any soldier
on a plain or hidden in a forest,
Trosler had to count on luck to spare him,
save him from the gunfire from his own side.
Going home with just a minor face wound
must have pleased even a would-be martyr
such as he. Like any common soldier
in the field, I'll bet, he wasn't certain,
often, where he was, or where he should be,
or how long he'd have to watch for muskets
pointing at him through the trees and bushes,
or what he was trying to accomplish
when he ordered his brigade to rush forth
into grapeshot. I was always worrying
what would happen to my keys and seegars
when I dove for cover. What concerned me,
more than being blown apart, was losing
those expensive, hand-rolled Cuban seegars
I had brought from New York. What do I care,
now that I've survived, for Cuban seegars?
Filthy things they are! They make your head spin.

At the time that Trosler made his way south,
I was living in New York, near Broadway,
not in Philadelphia. I'd gone there
to enlist . . . . Well, that's not why I'd gone there;
why I'd gone there is another story.
When I joined the 75th New Yorkers,
I had no idea that eight months later
I'd be living in New Orleans, keeping
detailed records, playing judge and jury
for unwieldy recruits, running errands
back and forth to Carrollton for Weitzel,
confiscating homes, including Bressie's.
Unattached and unaccountable,
I strolled from my room one autumn morning,
caught the omnibus down Broadway, walked in

to the War Department office, signed up,
and received my first commission — *Captain*.
That would be my first, and only, title.
There's no hero, no triumphant nation,
no immortal acts, no famous battles
glossing these long pages. Even Trosler
wasn't Herculean. He was modern.
This is 1868. So trust me.
My long-windedness discloses justly
what I take as truth.

6

Imagine next, then,
Bandeaux back in Bressie's garden, chatting,
gossiping of this or that, resisting,
making a fuss of everything but that thing
foremost in his mind. The tolerance
Bressie shows him, I suspect, reveals her . . .
how to put it? . . . her ambivalence,
so appealing in a woman. See her
sitting with him, hands crossed on her lap,
head bent slightly forward, green eyes tranquil,
as she listens to him with the patience
of a well-bred child? See how Bandeaux —
knowing how his cousin always holds fast,
weakens, then capitulates in other,
less important matters — complicates things?
Like a spider weaving webs around her,
he insists that she must come with him
to a certain inn a certain morning
several days from now. And she abides him,
giving less thought to his invitation
than to how his barrel-chested body,
hunch-backed, small-earred, pigeon-toed, reminds her,
with its legs crossed in the shade, of a pumpkin
when it struggles with a vine for sunlight.
Then she banishes the thought.

But later
Cupid couldn't be more pleased than Bandeaux
when he takes his niece to Touro's, feeds her
(royally, I suspect), then just happens,
as they linger in the sun, to notice

Trosler strutting down Canal on horseback!

"Gracious! What's that cheering? Come see, Bressie!
Look! It's Colonel White!"

And Bressie sees him.
She is not surprised by his appearance,
but like Mr. Crusoe, who said nothing
after months of scanning the horizon,
she gasps and is silent. Still, she sees him.
He's a man, she thinks, as though the others
riding next to him are flies. A blindness
lifts from her like a morning haze. Her chest heaves,
forcing from her lungs a sigh, and with it
every future she has been expecting
seems suspended from that balcony
like a wild palmetto leaf, as Trosler,
who by now has almost lost her image,
dismounts confidently to the banquette
where he's greeted by a crowd.

Imagine
Trosler, still oblivious to Bressie.
See that grapeshot scar across his cheek bone?
It's just half an inch below his right eye!
See his hands gesticulate in earnest
as he tells the *True Delta* his story
while, like Caesar home from Britain, he nods
at familiar faces on Canal Street —
merchants, store clerks, men of color, lawyers,
those he's known since childhood? Hear him spell out
carefully the name of every rider
of the Louisiana Eighth, his lips un-
furled beneath his mustache, hair pomaded,
shoulders squared? And as he stands there, erect,
not suspecting Bressie's presence, Bressie
sees his masculinity uncluttered
by the neutral laws that sex imposes.
Like a man who fixes his attention
on his watch, as he attempts to set it
accurately, carefully, precisely,
Trosler seems engaged in time, and happy.

At this moment, she begins to want him —
not at once: It doesn't come that quickly,

or at least for Bressie it comes slowly.
But within her stirs that sense of touching,
pressing her warm flesh against another's,
feeling a surge of blood beneath the surface
as it rushes on toward life, toward nothing.
She is his now.

That's how she explained it:
to observe him totally unhindered
by his own observing her. That moment —
illusory, suspended, incomplete,
briefer than the time it takes to tell it —
transformed Bressie's mind before she knew it,
and the months, the years, of living with it
afterwards could never root it out.
Surgery to amputate an arm
can't destroy its function, so the mind thinks.
And for years poor amputees continue
grasping after common objects, haunted
by the air that fills the empty spaces.

In the midst of conversation, Trosler,
glancing at the balcony, saw Bressie,
though he couldn't know that she had seen *him*.
Visibly unchanged, his stern demeanor
hardly showed the strain. But he had seen her.
And once that line between the two was drawn
what she had observed before was gone.

7

Here my speculations and my story
separate. At Helen's New Year's dinner.
Maybe how I think it happened isn't.
Maybe Bandeaux was behind the whole thing.
Maybe Bressie acted coyly. Maybe
Trosler did get sick. How to be certain?
I've decided that what Bressie told me
I should risk to writing. So I'll mix them
like a stew, her story and my hunches,
her potatoes and my carrots. Whether
by the end your skepticism waxes
or you judge me wrong, I can't determine.
Bressie, trying to solicit friendship,

shared what she thought I would never betray.
Now I am betraying her by writing.
Now I'll get it wrong. But does that matter?
Memory is only what we make it.
As for her place, don't presume her nature
"natural" because it is a woman's.
It's not easy to explain to others
what desire demands of us. And those who,
as it happens, are desire's objects
can't see clear to any explanation,
even should my effort to explain last
years, or pages. So like slaves on masters,
we depend on confidence and kindness,
our affinities.

Apparently, then,
Bandeaux made two moves, deliberately,
to draw Trosler closer to his cousin
(and, I guess, himself). As Bressie told it,
he brought tidings shortly after Christmas.
This alarmed her. (Always at holidays
one has time to be alarmed, with leisure
to guess why. A thoughtless, offhand comment,
usually ignored, takes on the drama
of Ideas.)

By now, at his discretion
Bandeaux would drop by to visit. He was,
he said, Bressie's "*époux protecteur*"
who felt free, more aptly, "obligated"
to inspect her private things, her habits,
her emotions, and even her bedroom,
where, he said, he must assess her clothing,
jewelry, linens, draperies, and toilet.
Bressie watched him rummage through her armoire.
What was he in search of among her corsets
and those parlor dresses she had not worn
for years? Should she toss him out with them?
Like the war itself, his strange behavior
so alarmed her she said almost nothing
but just watched him finger her silk linens.
Why should she care? How could Bandeaux harm her
more than her father had already?
She decided he was weak and foppish.
She was wrong.

One day he went to Trosler
to remind him of what he had promised
and how flabbergasted Bressie had been
to discover that the colonel knew her.

"Just as I predicted," Bandeaux added,
tossing both hands sideways with a shrug.
He suggested Trosler write to Bressie:
"This is Christmas. Why not send her greetings?
Tell her in your own words how you know her,
how I guessed from your precise description
who she was, how much it matters to you,
during these hard times, these trying times,
that she have your care and your protection.
Don't be shy. I'll guarantee an answer."

"I can't do that," Trosler laughed, then grimaced,
"I'm not good with words. Ashamed to write her.
Put me on a wild horse, a rapids
or a battlefield, before you ask me
to attempt a letter to a woman.
I am better silent."

"That's just perfect!
Don't you see, *ami*?"

"Is perfect? What is?"

"What you said, how you're ashamed to write her,
not too good with words, that horse talk. That's it.
Just be honest."

Trosler was persuaded,
not by reason, but by charm, to write her.
Tutored, tantalized and tugged by Bandeaux,
he got worked up to the point of over-
emphasizing, over-dramatizing
things he felt for one he'd seen only twice.
When one humid day out in her garden
we talked of her past, she joked about it,
ridiculed that letter for its phrasing
which, she claimed, used words more like a doctor's
than a poet's. She began to cite some —
melancholy, fever, sorrow's leeches,
heart's disease — words that show Trosler warming

vigorously to his project.
Surely,
I can't blame him. Done in isolation,
writing is a silent act that calls for
sheer extremes — breast beatings, cries of anguish,
overstated promises exploding
from an empty page. I always temper
critical remarks on others' writings,
especially those by men or women
mired in the feelings of their bodies,
since my own emotions when I'm writing
tend to soar like ducks out of a puddle.
Yet when Bressie laughed at Trosler's letter
I was quick, too quick, to go along.
Stupidly, I teased her.

"Men are such fools,"
I said, thinking somehow I was not one,
"How could you be serious about him
after such clichés? Do you still have it,
Trosler's letter? Why not read it to me
to instruct me on seducing women?"

"David! Why? How could you?" Bressie answered
and I knew I'd come on one of those moments
when you aren't the way you know you should be
but you are the way you are. Whatever
in the way of confidence I had gained,
hearing her account of Trosler, I lost,
once I drew attention to myself.
She did not complain, though. She stopped talking.
After a long pause, she changed the subject.
That explains why I can't quote that letter.
Had I been more eager to defend it —
taking his side and, against all reason,
arguing the case of hapless lovers —
Bressie might have listened, disagreed,
then gone upstairs to retrieve the letter,
taking me along. But as it happened,
though she was embarrassed by the writing,
Bressie read it carefully, re-read it,
and bequeathed herself to him who wrote it.
Put *me* on a wild horse or rapids
where in time I might learn how to ride;
I can't fathom people. How I've tried.

8

With that letter (which, as Bressie told me,
caused her more concern and less amusement
than it seemed to later) Bandeaux brought her
word of how her status in New Orleans
was endangered. This she knew already
and would quickly have ignored, but Bandeaux
in his shrewd, inexorable manner,
saw fit to throw up his arms in panic:
"Dear girl, how can you continue living
with this, this threat, to your . . . situation?
Why, just yesterday I heard such gossip —
at that little tea shop, down on Chartres,
oh, you know the place, I'm sure, they have there
the most delicate bon-bons. This fellow —
name is, I think, Peter Polyphenos,
or like that, an enemy of Charles —
he wants, evidently, to bring charges
against the LaRouchés, says the daughter,
that would be you — he despises Charles —
says he thinks you should be sent in exile,
says since he's Confederate he's legal.
O I just can't understand their language.
Sick nunk property soon. Something like that.
I am worried silly!"

"Don't be, Uncle.
I believe I know that man. His two friends,
both their names begin with A, have backed him.
They've been aching to do harm to Father
ever since he wouldn't lend them money
for some business scheme in Mexico.
Now I guess they're after me, a widow.
Maybe they want me to pay them something
to stop hounding me. I have so little,
let them have it."

"No, no! We must stop them,"
Bandeaux said, as Bressie's color whitened,
"I have taken steps that should prevent them
ever from tormenting you. Already —
O, I know you don't mind, such a tizzy
I've been in these days, so much has happened
I've not had much chance to keep the art shop

from dissolving, going under, kaput!
What with all my artists *and* my patrons
running off, the money — "

"You were saying?"

"Yes, it's the materials I'm lacking . . .,
but, I've gone to Deveraux — you know him,
he's a chief advisor to the general,
says he knows you, says the general knows you
and thinks highly of you — he can help you.
He says he's delighted he'll be dining
New Year's Day at Helen's. Aren't you going?
You must go and talk with him yourself, dear.
Who knows who might be there — General Lovell,
others of some influence. You must go.
Tell them of this Polyphenos creature.
Tell them what you know."

"Well, maybe, uncle,"
Bressie answered thoughtfully, "Well, maybe.
Yes." The color rushed back to her cheeks.

"Then it's settled," Bandeaux said and grabbed her,
wrapping both his arms around her shoulders,
pulling her to him, "Just do as I say.
Things should work out perfectly for you."
Holding her behind the neck, he kissed her
hesitantly. Then as though not knowing
what to do with her, he leaned his face close,
grinning, lips drawn back exposing both gums
like a wolf's. "You'll see." He then released her,
fleeing her as though pursued by hunters.
Turning near the door, he said, "Tomorrow
I'll be back, once you have read that letter . . .
and you've written your reply."

Remember,
what I'm telling you is Bressie's version:
She went to her room and shut the door.
Never had she realized how imprisoned
men's affection made her feel. She sat down,
distantly, before her mirror. Shadows
from the dying afternoon, like old age,
crossed her face in silence. Then she dozed off.

When she woke to darkness, with her head pressed
into her crossed arms on her dressing table,
she recalled how she had fallen asleep
just like this two days before she married.
Turning to the mirror, to the changes
in her face from that time to the present,
she thought, **I look much the same. I'm older —
there are lines around my eyes, and dark spots —
but the rest seems much the same. I must change.
Help me. Help me.** Then she lit the gas lamp,
wrapped a shawl around her shoulders, lifted
from her drawer a sheet of writing paper,
and composed,

Dear Colonel White,
I'm flattered
by what you so eloquently wrote me
and can't hope to match its grace, but, sir, I,
who have every reason to be honored
by your deeply felt professions, cannot,
due to my viduity, receive them
in the terms you kindly offer . . .

Formal.
Written with restraint. How could a letter
written to a stranger to reject him,
written with such conscious poise and distance,
liberate its author? When I asked her,
her reply, as I recall, was lengthy,
her eyes darkening intensely, face flushed:
"I had written it myself. I realized
I was lonely, ready to be touched.
Any man would do, it seemed. But this time
there was no one there, no father, husband,
uncle, telling me to keep my distance
from what they would call my 'womanish' way.
Left alone, they feared — and I feared with them —
I might act irrationally, wildly,
as my mother had. But . . . this was *my* choice.
Did I want this man to touch my body
where he might unleash its demons, free them
like shore birds that haven't learned to fly yet.
Or did I feel free myself to do it,
to release them, on my own? The question
was not whether I found him attractive —

his array, his look, his heart, his person,
his gentility all seemed appealing —
but I longed to make my own decisions,
to move through my skin by *my* volition,
to be womanish *and* free, not driven.
So that letter, though it sounded formal,
even prudish to my uncle, wasn't.
It did not express rejection, anger,
love, fear, nor indifference towards Trosler.
It protected me from my desire
yet it kept it near at hand. It's simple.
Trosler's anger I could risk, his kindness
I had lived for thirty years not knowing,
but to move myself — how could he know this? —
to exist in my own blood, to breathe whole,
as you might go swimming with your clothes off
giving yourself over to the water
with affinity, how wonderful then
just to be a human being being.
So I wrote him with the concentration
of a child playing children's games."

Bandeaux, when he came to fetch this letter,
chortled at his niece's mood. He teased her,
twinkling, "Seems you find the Christmas season,
shall we say, agreeable? I'm so pleased
you've seen fit to satisfy the Colonel.
Was his greeting friendly?"

"I responded,
as you asked. I told him I support him
in his work for peace and independence.
As his sister, I shall share in these things."

"Sister? Charming! How divine!" quipped Bandeaux,
"He'll be satisfied, I'm sure." He smiled,
not unlike a buccaneer who smiles
when he eyes a silver-laden frigate
passing through his spyglass. With her letter
smuggled safely out in his coat pocket,
Bandeaux struck out boldly for St. Charles
like Lafitte, embarking for new quarrels.

9

As he read her letter, Trosler trembled.
Here had Bressie's hand been! These words, her words!
Meant for his eyes only! Words that told him
nothing he was not prepared to find there.
What he found was modesty and meekness,
and inspired by these, as he remembered
how she threw her head back at the opera,
his heart started beating, beating faster,
faster than the time he'd sat on horseback
waiting for the charge up Henry House Hill.
He re-read her letter three times, searching,
line by line, for words of hope and promise.
Starting in a fourth time, he was shadowed
by a growing sense of dread. He fought that,
slowly going over every sentence
patiently until, at last, he settled,
like a dog who finds a place for resting
after circling around a rug, on those spots
which had first aroused a sense of comfort.
Still, the more he read, the more he wanted.
What she'd hoped would calm his apprehensions
had instead inflamed them. He could taste her,
almost. He was sure that she was modest,
not aloof.

But then he turned to Bandeaux:
"Why is she not more direct? As I was?
I'm confused. Your niece says — "

"Colonel! Colonel!"
Bandeaux interrupted, as he sidled
over to him like a village preacher,
putting one hand on this sinner's shoulder,
"Don't fly off the handle. This is nothing,
just a woman's natural defenses
so you won't feel too much confidence.
Once they've fallen, women can do nothing,
and this woman's obviously fallen.
Why, if you don't think so, just keep hacking
like a woodsman. She may sense the danger.
Can you blame her? She may seem to flatter,
while at bottom she stays rooted, nay, stuck
in a cold denial. But remember,

every oak tree seems secure and steadfast
as the woodsman hacks at it. It stands proud.
But in one clean, happy stroke it crashes
while the woodsman revels in his harvest.
Just keep hacking." Bandeaux gripped his forearm,
pressing Trosler to his chest, "and tell me,
if you trust me, how I might prove useful
to this enterprise. With some investment
you may reap a profit you have never,
never dared dream of: You've been invited,
by my instigation, to a dinner
New Year's evening in the Anglo District.
Colonel Deveraux, I think you know him — "

"Deveraux! I trust him more than any,"
Trosler said, then looking down at Bandeaux
added, "Other than my cousin, that is,
er, and you. What of him?"

"If you're willing,
I might easily arrange a moment . . .
how can I best put this? Words of love are,
monsieur, *très complexe*. But should you want to,
you might have brief intercourse with Bressie
for yourself. I have it on good hearsay
she must ask your Deveraux a favor,
just a little family problem, mind you,
but, if you're there, Deveraux and I might — "

"What? I can't do that! I'm too embarrassed
after what I wrote. It's much too public.
Leave me to the horses. They will need me,
that night, at Camp Walker."

"Don't speak nonsense.
I have no intention of assigning
you the fool's role. That's for me," joked Bandeaux,
"Listen, if you follow my suggestion,
I assure you, Bressie will seek *you* out.
No one, none but I, will overhear you.
Privacy," he whispered, and again,
"Privacy. If you do what I tell you."

There he goes, you're thinking, **making Trosler mindless. How can he know? He's just jealous,**

painting Southerners as unctuous jackals.
Maybe. I have tried to keep my envy
out of this. And all my sources tell me —
even Bressie — Bandeaux was a scoundrel,
mephistophelian. But forgive me.
Maybe he said, "Piracy" or "Try me."
Maybe Trosler paid him no attention.
Fine. But Bressie dined at Helen's that night.
Trosler went to bed in Helen's guest room.
And, much later, during stormy weather,
weren't the two of them in bed together?

10

Most Orleanians slept past eleven
New Year's morning. But not Mansfield Lovell.
It was 1862. As usual,
after breakfast at six, he went downtown
to receive the War Department envoy.
All day he attended to his papers —
troop recruitments, ammunition records,
cannons for Forts Jackson and St. Philip,
railroad schedules, steamer reconversions,
field reports from scouts along the Gulf Coast,
camp requests for uniforms and rations.
Then at three he rode out to Camp Walker
to inspect the barracks, guard-posts, foundries,
shipyard, and stockade. At seven-thirty
his assisting officers assembled
for their daily staff report, which Lovell,
as he listened, might revise. Exceptions,
such as illness or a field assignment,
were allowed, especially on New Year's.
Most of Lovell's officers were absent
this night, still recovering, it seems,
so at ten, exhausted, Lovell walked home,
supped on chicken, scribbled out a letter,
posted it to Beauregard, and turned in
early.

Similarly, Helen Clairborne,
while the city slept late, roused her servants —
Cassie Mae the cook and Jacques the butler —
took her breakfast, then drove down to market

to find the best poultry, meats and fresh greens
she could for her dinner: mutton, chicken,
veal, a ham, potatoes, eggplants, turnips,
cauliflower, and a pumpkin. Later
she went to the wharf to buy the oysters,
terrapin, tilapia, and fish heads
Cassie Mae would need to make a gumbo.
Helen was as famous in New Orleans
for her *grandes affaires* as Bandeaux was.
All day back and forth across her courtyard
she ran, from the main house to the kitchen
and back, as she supervised the cooking,
testing oysters for their tenderness,
stirring the stock, adding clumps of peppers
to the gumbo, trimming mutton fat, or
watching Cassie beat the veal, then snapping,
"Get rid of those eyes, boy!" at the cook's help,
as he lazily peeled each potato.
(Then once Helen stepped out, Cassie Mae said,
waxing philosophic, "Do as she say.
White folk, dey doan like no food to watch'em
whiles dey eatin'. Cut dem big ol' eyes out
or Miz Helen she might scare her own kin.")
Later, Helen picked out from her wine rack
choice Madeiras put their by her husband,
champagne he'd brought from the Soissons region,
and for pousse-café, an Otard brandy.

Next, at three o'clock she bathed. Two hours
she spent, powdering herself, then curling
out her hair, then tying on her corset,
trying seven petticoats to find one
she was satisfied with, dabbing perfume,
rouge and kohl onto her pale pink features —
she was also well-known for her eyebrows,
joined and narrow, delicate, exquisite!
Then, enveloping her perfumed body
in a yellow sarcenet gown, lovely
as a glimpsed Eurydice descending,
she, at eight precisely, went downstairs
and began to greet her guests:

First, Bandeaux,
who was always early to a party,
then those two young women, dressed in white,

who had like snow been draped on Bressie's lawn chairs,
Tarba and Toinette, who both said nothing,
gliding in like unexpected breezes.
Next came Trosler, Deveraux, then others
who'd been granted this night free by Lovell.
One, I gather, was a Colonel Johnson,
always sporting his black Cuban seegar;
also, Captains Townsend and Montgomery,
recently returned from Richmond; others,
maybe. Let's skip these preliminaries.
We'll say Bressie came unusually late.
None, save God, the stars, and Bandeaux, knew then
he or she'd been asked there for a reason
other than to pass a pleasant evening.
Bressie was an innocent, so she claimed.
Frolic, she said, was the standing order,
since most thought the war would soon be over,
setting free the whole Confederacy,
so when Trosler took aside his hostess
and confided that he had a headache,
Helen naturally believed the party
New Year's Eve at the St. Louis had caused it.

"Oh," she cooed, "Won't you come here and lie down?"
guiding Trosler to her guest room. "Poor man,
let me grab a compress," she said, smiling
one of those dismissive, frigid smiles
Southern women are so famous for.
Trosler, though, soon dropped into a deep sleep
getting more rest in that hour or two
than he'd had for weeks. So Helen left him,
anxious to return to her guests' pleasure.

Meanwhile in the foyer, Bandeaux mingled,
as the guests approached their seats for dinner.
Spotting Deveraux — a red-faced young man
not yet round but with a double chin
who was joking with Toinette and Tarba —
Bandeaux proclaimed, "Look! The Lord of Hades,
flanked by Demeter and Proserpine!"

Deveraux grinned devilishly, "Fine, fine.
But whatever grain they grow is mine, *oui*?"

Bandeaux snickered, then moved one step closer,

as he quickly turned the conversation
from Greek goddesses to war: "So, Colonel,
what chance is there that the war will end soon,
now that we have driven Lincoln's army
to the border? Will you break this blockade?
It's distressing to feel *so* imprisoned,
don't you know? You *can* talk freely, can't you?"

Everyone, like creatures in a forest
when they think they've heard a rattlesnake, paused,
sniffing out the danger, then resumed
their activities — unruffling napkins,
pulling chairs out, tinkling glasses, chatting —
as though Bandeaux's words had lost their echo.

Once the moment had passed, Deveraux said,
"Victory is ours. No doubt about it,"
as he watched them bring the soup tureen in,
ladle and serve, "As for Lincoln's cretins,
all we need to do is choose the right time
to take Washington — through Maryland, say —
and to bring McClellan to us begging,
begging for peace. But, no need to hurry.
Time is on our side." He slurped his gumbo,
joining the muted chorus of full soup spoons.
"Mmmm, delicious!"

"Yes, it's scrumptious, Madam,"
Captain Townsend pitched in from the far side,
"How they lack delectables in Richmond
like this. But, if I might disagree, sir,
I say we should act immediately,
not wait for the North to reconnoiter."
Pausing, he watched Jacques remove his soup dish.
"I say we advance now."

"That's sheer horse talk!"
Deveraux said, "Look at our objectives.
We're not the invaders. We attack now,
and we lose the confidence of England
we have worked so carefully to foster.
No, like alligators, we need patience.
Cotton will prevail for us. The British,
once the summer comes, will feel their losses.
Then you'll see, friend, what they think of Lincoln."

"Man talk," Helen groaned, "The losses I see
are right here," and nodding at her wine glass,
she arranged a smile.

"Of course. A toast, then,"
Deveraux announced, abruptly standing,
"To the honor of Louisiana!
Union, Justice, Confidence! Forever
may they shine as at this hour!"

"Here, here,"
Bandeaux chimed in, "May they always prosper.
But, let's not forget our charming hostess."

"Yah!" barked Colonel Johnson, "What a great feast!
I have always had a taste for pressed veal.
Madam." Rising, he kicked his chair over
but he quickly righted it again.

Tarba and Toinette began to giggle.
Then, as Jacques began to serve the mutton,
Bandeaux said, "And surely, we're not finished.
I must also toast our brave defenders,
all these gentlemen who grace our presence,
as we start the new year — all, that is, but — "
and he paused, "— but B.T. White."

"Poor Trosler,"
Helen sighed, "He's ill."

"My brother Trosler?"
piped in Deveraux, and as all listened,
he began to diagnose the headache
which was keeping *Le Blanc Américain*
from their fete. Indeed, throughout the dinner,
in between the compliments to Helen,
each guest offered his, or her, suggestion
as to how to aid their friend, while Helen,
who seemed quite pleased now, took note of each one
with a condescending smile. With each bite
came more remedies — except from Bressie
who, because she had the cure, kept silent.

Eagerly attending this discussion,
Bandeaux turned to Captain Townsend. "Please, sir,

something you said earlier disturbed me.
When you said we should press forward, what then?
That is, what will happen when we do win?
What will we demand of them?"

"Of Yankees?"

"And their sympathizers."

"They're barbaric!
Look at how that bastard Wilkes behaved
when he snatched the *Trent*, Slidell and Mason.
What a pack of vipers! And what's worse is
most think Wilkes was much too easy on them.
Northern journalists say Wilkes lacks courage,
say he should have rammed and sunk that packet.
That's why I say now's the time to sally,
while the world is with us."

"Take revenge, then?"

"Certainly."

"But what of suspect persons,. . .
like my niece here?"

Once again a silence,
briefly, like the silence after lightning,
fell across the room.

"She's an exception!"
thundered Deveraux across the table,
"I assure you, Bressie's not a problem."

"What's her case?" Montgomery inquired.

As the butler circled, filling glasses,
Bandeaux told the tale of Polyphenos
and his cruel designs.

"She's innocent,"
was Montgomery's verdict.

Townsend rallied,
"Innocent as New Year's Day. As we are,

victims of those worshippers of Mammon.
Anyone can see."

"And Colonel Johnson?"
Bandeaux asked, "Do you accept their judgement?"

Putting down his fork and leaning backwards,
Johnson laid a hand across his stomach,
stared into his empty plate, and muttered,
"Well, since you ask me, I think she's lucky
having friends like you who can protect her,
put a good word in. The military,
in its wisdom, frankly, all too often
overlooks those who are too unworldly
to protect themselves."

"My point exactly,"
Bandeaux said and started picking pie crumbs
from the tablecloth, "Who, when the time comes,
will be there to stand up for this poor girl
once the war is over?"

"I know *I* shall,"
said Montgomery.

"All of us should swear to!"
Townsend shouted, quickly standing upright,
lifting his wine glass and kicking his heels.

Bressie, feeling heat rise through her backbone,
kept her eyes averted from her saviors.

"Gentlemen," said Helen, dully, "Thank you.
Shall we all withdraw into the parlor?
Coffee? Brandy? Seegars?"

"*Un moment*, dear,"
Bandeaux pressed on, "First I must ask you, sir —
Colonel Deveraux — just one last question.
I was wondering if Colonel Trosler . . .,
surely, he'd agree with all of you here,
isn't he the best one to petition
to insure she isn't inconvenienced.
Bressie, I mean. He has Lovell's ear, yes?"

"Grand idea! A workable suggestion."

"But . . . he's ill," said Helen. Then she smiled,
cautiously, at Deveraux.

"That's nothing,"
Bandeaux reassured her, "Once he hears this,
he'll be much improved, in my opinion."

"Patience. Let me ask him first. Now please, sirs,
let's retire. The coffee's cold." She waited
as each chair returned was punctuated.

11

Slipping from the hall into the guest room,
Helen tiptoed up to Trosler, resting
comfortably on his back, his head propped
by three pillows, with his right arm slung up
overhead, the compress on his eyelids.
Carefully, in order not to wake him,
she reached across to fluff up the pillow
on his left side, then removed the compress
gently, steadying him with her right hand.
Pausing, bending even closer to him,
she thought, **How he's dreaming!** and she marveled
at his tiny mustache hairs, the red skin
where his cheek was scarred, the narrow lips
tightly closed, as though they had been ordered
by some officer to sleep in silence.
What experience, she mused, **has melded
such determination with such beauty?**

Then, awakened by her heady perfume,
Trosler stirred. She had both arms around him.
"Why, excuse me. I have not disturbed you,
have I?" Helen whispered, "I just couldn't,
could I, let this damp old compress chill you?"

"Fine. I'm fine. I'm fine," said Trosler, thinking
with what little consciousness he had
how he might stretch out his arm and shift it
without touching Helen's breast or thigh.
Pause.

Helen watched him clench his teeth. "Much better,
are we?" she politely asked and smiled,
maybe too politely. Trosler nodded,
which gave her a chance to lift her arms out
delicately from behind the pillows.
Then, withdrawing so fast from the bedside
you might think she'd only moved in spirit,
leaving her sweet body, full and fragrant,
clinging there to Trosler's chest, she asked him,
"By the way, would you be greatly troubled
if my guest here — Bandeaux — brought his niece in.
She might have a question. Her name's Bressie."

"Bressie?" **How much does she know?** He panicked.

"Pshaw! Don't feel embarrassed. You look splendid.
There's no need to dress. She knows you're not well.
Bandeaux wants to ask a favor, that's all.
Just a moment."

Helen stepped out. Trosler,
jumping from the bed, brushed back his hair slick
with his fingers. Then he smoothed the blanket,
as though feeling for that part of Helen
left behind. He quickly tucked his shirt in,
crawled back into bed, and waited, breathless.
In walked Bandeaux.

"*Mon ami*," he whispered,
as he danced across the room and giggled,
"Here she comes!" He straightened Trosler's collar.
In walked Helen. Then behind her, Bressie.
Trosler wished his hair were not so messy.

12

Why should I go on? There is no reason
I should tell how Trosler looked at Bressie,
how, though scared, he felt his sex stir somewhere
underneath the quilt, how she felt naked
meeting his glance with her dark eyes. No one
in that room believed, quite, in the others —
gathered there like strangers in a stagecoach
thrown inconsequentially together,

crossing some inconsequential prairie
until, inadvertently, some light breeze
passes through the coach, so that for years
none of them forgets that idle crosswind,
even as its image fades, its sunset
turns to dawn, the strangers' faces brighten
into those of friends, the breeze itself grows
more intense, its gale-force winds approaching.

Blindess keeps from me the sight of Bressie
smiling warmly at her suitor, smiling
at his meager "Well. Now." Here there's nothing
for a chronicler to burst with words for.
Why should I tell how each of them acted,
where exactly Bressie's nervous hands went
as she introduced herself, how Helen
often gestured toward the bed, how Bandeaux
later left them to themselves, the color
flushing into Trosler?

Blindness keeps me.
You must trust me, though I am not honest.
Deaf ears save me hearing Bandeaux's chatter
rushing forth, a broken dam that floods them,
splashing Bressie toward the bed and Trosler.
I can't hear their words, what passed between them.
I refuse to —

Davenport, be careful!
Senses other than your sight and hearing
rise in you, distorting things that matter:
Face it. Trosler touched her hands before you,
tasted her lips and smelled her skin, as Bressie,
standing in the room of her one close friend,
tugged between one stranger and another,
with her independence gone, forgotten
like a loved one dead these three years,
dangled.
Shall I leave her in this other's shadow,
heart and appetite suspended, darkness
pleasing as the light? And what of Trosler,
sad receptacle of all that's passing?

I'll complete this history. I promise.
I'll go on. But I must stop now, tired.

I must leave the two of them together,
he reclining, she half in the distance,
half nearby. It's Sunday. Time for walking.
Then tomorrow work. I have a long week,
then a month of weeks ahead with papers,
stacks of Bureau papers I must finish,
as though such a task were terminable,
signing freedmen, teaching them the new laws.
This is my work now. I'm sorry, Trosler.
Stay in bed. Enjoy your lover's seizure.
I'll unleash your rapture at my leisure.

DAVENPORT'S VERSION

BOOK III

1

Union, Justice, Confidence. The credo
of the people of Louisiana.
Virtue, Liberty and Independence.
Pennsylvania's credo. Kindness? Nowhere.
So where does a government liaison,
one paid as a go-between between two
spent and bleeding nations, turn to?

Union?
Who can give me power to inspire
union, peace or hope, among survivors?
I can't bring back horses to their owners,
stolen whisky, confiscated silver.
I can't teach the Negroes all the letters
of the law, nor guarantee their safety
from their cunning former overseers.
How can I pretend to settle matters
outside my control? How comfort women
husbands have abandoned? Gather taxes?
Clear up property disputes? Spare children
from those parents who would sell them?

Justice?
Where is justice when an army comes in
and disrupts the local way of life?
Those of us, like ants, who boarded troop ships
and then ran the log jam at Fort Jackson,
fancied we were harbingers of justice:
Virtue. Abolition. Independence.
How perceptions change in seven years.
Traveling with Farragut upriver,
we thought we would "liberate" the Negroes,
so, like ants, since we had made our minds up,
steadily we came, the rank and file,
justice the munitions in our weapons,
justice in the guise of cannon powder,

musket balls and grapeshot. No one stopped us.
Later, heading north, we would replace it,
justice, with the plunder from plantations,
hordes of freed slaves, and a swarm of problems —
what to feed the freedmen, where to house them,
how to enforce the Oath of Allegiance,
when to pardon rebels, when to bleed them,
when to send them back out to their canefields
on their own.

Does Confidence from Justice
follow? Does fidelity from pride?
We can raise the Federal flag, protect it,
hang Confederates, hang sympathizers
like that fool who climbed the Mint House flagpole,
hang all those who speak, and call that "justice."
We can do as Butler did and fake laws
to accommodate our momentary,
mercantile designs, and call that "justice."
We can strip warehouses, sell off steamers,
occupy the fugitives' plantations,
drink up all their wine, and call that "justice."
We can apprehend the local women,
white and black, demand their full allegiance,
terrorize them to find out their secrets,
burn their houses down, and call that "justice."
But what imagery does confidence stir?
Rows and rows of hospital cots for the dying
who had cheerfully marched off to battle?
Pale-faced mistresses, huddled with servants
when we found them, often in their cisterns?
When we'd ask them what goods they had buried,
they swore they had nothing hid, were loyal,
and would gladly serve our every need,
if we promised not to torch their cotton,
steal their horses and destroy their cattle,
all in the name of justice?

Or my landlord
leaning on the doorframe of my chamber
when I first moved in, and saying, "Captain,
we feel *so much* safer, now that you're here,
all you Yankees," as he rubbed his bald head
with a greasy palm and, leering, eyed me
as though I were vermin.

Trust me, reader.

Though I am not honest, still there's kindness.
I won't mention love, since love is mindless
and absurd. Love is as transitory
as a spring flood, not unlike this story.

2

Now, where was I? 1862. Yes?
Helen's house. With Trosler propped in bed there.
Bressie standing near in her finest clothes —
black merino waist, a sash of satin,
silver brooch, pearl earrings, pleated black skirt —
shades of kohl around her eyes, now darkened
as she turns her head away from Bandeaux
(who has left the door ajar) to Trosler,
nervous Trosler. Squinting in the gaslight
to examine her, to trace her secrets,
crack her code, he fixes her. She meets him,
eye to eye, in the winter's evening shadows.
What was it he'd planned to say? What was it
late that night he couldn't sleep near Memphis
had he pledged he'd say to Bressie later,
if the Lord would only let him survive?
How could he forget? How be so stupid?

So he searches Bressie's eyes, their corners.
It's as though they hold his answers.

She says,
"Colonel White. I hope you're feeling better."

"Yes. Oh. Better. Thank you." And his thick legs,
stretched beneath the comforter, seem trapped there
as though underneath a fallen horse,
such is the male instinct to be standing
in the company of women.

"Good, then."

In the middle of the room, her figure,
silhouetted by the fire and gaslight,
is as dark and vivid as a lighthouse
seen from sea, when its beacon has burned low —
isolated from both shore and ocean.

Scanning the room, Trosler seeks a chair
for her. In one corner near the basin
sits a mora. Throwing off his blanket,
he leaps from the bed and grabs it. "Take this."
Then he sets it three feet from the bed.

"No,"
Bressie now responds, "Stay still, don't bother . . ."
Taking his arms, gently she directs him
back to bed, but not before he, deftly
reaching around her waist, pulls the mora
slightly closer, as though he's expecting
furniture to do his talking for him —
Helen's tall four-poster and this footstool.

"I am not uncomfortable," she says,
but she then sits down, her knees together
as she twists her legs to one side, skirt
tucked beneath her thighs, while Trosler watches.
Smoothing both her palms across her lap,
she looks up at Trosler, partly standing,
partly leaning backwards on a pillow.
"I must thank you," she says, "for your letter."

Trosler digs his fists into the bedclothes.
"No, that's not — "

But Bressie smiles, "What's not?"

Trosler sighs and both his fists sprout fingers,
taking root in Helen's quilt. His weight shifts.
"Nothing," he says, parting his teeth once more
but behind closed lips. He beckons to her
with his eyes, then looks away.

"For kindness,"
Bressie says, "I feel indebted to you."

Trosler shivers. **That was not my meaning.**
Why does she not understand? Withdrawing,
he leans further back against the bedpost,
wishing it were she. But Bressie does know
what he meant, so why is she resisting?
Not so fast, she hears her mind reciting
to itself, the centuries behind her,

centuries of women's self-protection,
not so fast. She holds her breath a moment
as though she might still this room, this fire
offering its heat and narrow half-light.

Silence, as the two of them recover.
Like a juggler who drops one of his balls
but continues tossing through the thin air
those balls still in motion, quite ignoring,
whether by resolve or by obsession,
this disruption, Trosler reaches forward,
taking Bressie's hand in his: "Believe me,
I . . ., I . . ." Bressie starts to breathe again. "I,
I have felt so mad, being so stupid.
But I'm not mad. I am only stupid."

"Sir, I don't know what you want."

"You call me
'Sir' or 'Colonel.' You embarrass me so.
All I ask . . ., is there a chance that we might . . .
meet? To talk together? I have something . . ."

(Well. I must intrude here. Trosler's nervous
so he pleads with Bressie like a child
trying to get its mother to embrace it.
But the difference is that Trosler, seated,
leaning forward, holding Bressie's hand,
towers over her. He's like a live oak,
neither twitch nor quiver in his posture.
Let his childish way, his awkward manner,
not obscure the power of his body,
eyes and eyebrows black against his white cheeks,
brawny neck, broad shoulders, sturdy forearms,
large hands that can calm a horse and tame it
with caresses, slender hips and strong legs.
He, in short, is beautiful to Bressie,
not as children are but as a man is.)

"Bressie, I had hoped to gain your favor.
But now look at me. Half on my knees. And,"
glancing back, he sees the twisted bedclothes
hanging from the bed, half-wrapped around him,
"I can think of nothing else but you."

Bressie puts her right hand on his forehead:
"Don't be sad. I too am taken."

"Are you?"

"Yes," she laughs, "Of course. But I don't know you."

"Don't be nervous. I'm not usually
so — " he looks around, "so careless." Rising,
he picks up the bedclothes. "Help me, won't you,
fix these blankets?"

They arrange the bed
silently together. Trosler sits down.
Then he stands again.

"I'm sorry," he says.

"Why?" she asks.

"I guess I should be going."

"Acting like a little boy," I grumbled,
"That's one of the oldest tricks. It can't miss
if the woman is entangled with you,
but if she withdraws, how silly you look."

"Don't you think I know that? You're some expert,
David Davenport. Do not most women,
in their own way, use the same maneuver?
Play into the other's strength. Disarm him."

"Why give in, then?"

"I did *not* give in! Ah!
Can't you see that? Why would I resist him?
Damn your arrogance. What of those long months
wasted, wasted? Trosler gone off, fighting,
while I waited out the war in silence
like the party dresses in my armoire,
waiting to be eaten by the moths!
Oh, it's fine for me to nurse the children
orphaned by the war, or I may follow,
in the newspapers, the daily carnage.
No one stops me running off and joining

this brigade of whores — or that of horses!
No one cares!"
                                        She banged her fists against me.
"I'm a woman. I change nothing, nothing.
I can't stop the carnage. I can't father
fatherless ones. I can't melt your armor
into flesh, or soup, or waterlilies.
So a man's a child?"

                    "But Bressie?"

                                        "*So* what?
So I wanted him and let him have me
his way? Does that mean that I'm a witch?"

                                                  "No."

In my jealousy I couldn't hear her.
I am sorry now that I said nothing
more, but who was I then, but a loner
thirteen hundred miles from Pennsylvania
with its Virtue and its Independence,
thirteen hundred miles from the safety
of my cloistered life, who had no function
other than, it seemed, to play the spoiler?
No triumphant nation stood behind me
when I tried to take her in my arms:
Was I smothering her? Gently yielding,
she refused to cry, although I kissed her
and caressed her, as I might a child.
Then I slipped my hand between her thighs.

        Trosler, slumped, arms dangling from his shoulders
like two branches split by lightning, mumbles,
"It's all hopeless. May as well stop fighting.
We're the fox. We're hiding in the bushes.
They're the poachers. Can't you hear them coming,
beating on the ground behind us? I can.
They will smoke us out, I tell you."

                                        "Trosler,"
Bressie says, "I'm yours."

                                        "I heard no answer,"
Bandeaux chirps, his head stuck through the doorway,

"Did you hear my knocking? *Tout va bien, non?*"
Then he whispers, "Bressie, we must go now.
Tell me first, though," and he whisks up to her,
turns his back to Trosler, lifts his hands up
to her cheeks, and pulls her face to his,
"Have you settled anything between you?"
Then he spies the lines below her dark eyes.
"Yes! I knew it!" he exclaims. On one cheek,
smack! he kisses her, then turns to Trosler,
"I'm so pleased for both of you."

"I guess so,"
Trosler mutters.

"I'm so pleased to see you
finally united. My achievement,
if I say so myself."

"Yes," sighs Bressie,
"after what has happened here tonight
I can put my faith in Colonel White."

3

Voices in the hallway. Helen enters.
With her Colonel Deveraux.

"Good night, sir,"
Bressie says to Trosler, then while turning,
"Thank you, Helen."

Helen doesn't hear her
since she's blushing from some indiscretion
Deveraux's apparently committed
just outside the door. She runs to Bressie,
slipping one arm underneath her friend's.
"Save me, dear!" she screeches, "Mister — Colonel —
Deveraux! Why, you are simply awful!
You would not believe . . ." He shrugs his shoulders,
innocently grinning at her. "Oh, my!"
Helen, fanning herself with her glove, adds,
"Men!" She smiles at Trosler. "Well, now, you two,
have you all discussed that business matter?"

“I’m about to leave,” says Bressie.

“Really?”
Deveraux says loudly, just too loudly,
“So am I. You feeling better, B.T.?
You’ve missed quite an evening — charming hostess,
lively crowd, you Anglos. And the brandy,
Mad’moselle, *parfait!*” He pats his stomach.
“But as I was saying in the hall there:
comes a time for bed and dreaming. Madam,
may I take you home?”

“How perfect! Perfect!”
Bandeaux interjects, “Sir, you’re a savior
more than you can know. If you take Bressie,
I can help this poor man to his bed.”

Trosler grimaces.

“Well, I don’t like it.”
Helen feigns a pout. “Not this arrangement.
You go off with this one, you with that one.
Who will stay with me? The evening’s young still.
Even children haven’t started dreaming.
Won’t you take another brandy? Colonel?”
Trosler looks at Bressie, but the banter —
first from Deveraux, then Bandeaux, Helen,
Bandeaux, Deveraux again, then Helen —
keeps her having to return his stare.

Then she says, “I’m grateful to you, Colonel.
Shall we?”

“Name’s René,” says Deveraux,
hand on her arm, as they turn to go.

4

Bandeaux, helping Trosler put his boots on,
quizzes him for details of the “visit.”
Now let’s see.

“She’s very sweet,” says Trosler.

"Sweet?" gasps Bandeaux in exasperation,
as he plops down on the bed beside him,
"Let me tell you what I know of Bressie.
She's *la crème de la crème*, my little cousin,
never disobeys, can't harm a creature
under God's blue heaven. I have known her,
I admit it, since she was a child.
Often, I would take her out — her father,
he's a famous man, a great physician —
and I've watched her like a cotton planter
supervising his fields. So if something,
anything, should happen to her, I'd feel,"
Bandeaux puts his hand on Trosler's shoulder,
"well, responsible. I couldn't leave her,
whom I think of as my wife, or daughter,
to just any smartly dressed young sabreur,"
as his hand to Trosler's other shoulder
slips, and he leans even closer to him,
"Men, you know," he whispers, "are such braggarts.
Deveraux, for instance, with his manner
so appropriate when chatting with women,
his smooth Creole charm, his hair and mustache
neatly clipped, his boots oiled, and his silk gloves
not worn at the trigger finger. Such men,
when no woman is around to stop them,
can plunge from the pinnacle of virtue
to the most lascivious . . ., I've known some,
some who, when with other men," his voice drops
to a murmur, "over rum and seegars,
boast about extraordinary things —
how Miss So-and-so prefers her mornings
after tea, how many times they've done it,
visited the country cottage of a
certain general's mistress, or on what hills,
if they had the chance to, they would tittup
with a Lady S when she goes riding.
Quel choquant!" He shakes his head. "The scandal!"

"What are you suggesting? What?" asks Trosler,
"That I'll shame her? Too bad you don't know me.
I'm less likely to humiliate her
than Jeb Stuart would his cavalry,
Beauregard his Washington Artillery,
Alexander Macedonia!
Lies and rumors, boasts and degradation.

Image from “Farragut’s Fleet Passing the Forts Below New Orleans” by Mauritz F. H. DeHaas, ca. 1866. Historic New Orleans Collection.

“Bayou Plaquemines” by Joseph Rusling Meeker, 1881.
Courtesy of Ogden Museum of Southern Art.

Those are blasphemies." He likes saying that.
"Blasphemies, sir. I'm surprised you think me
capable of blasphemies."

"Of course not,"
Bandeaux says, his grin showing his bad teeth.

Slipping out from under his friend's clutches,
Trosler adds, "How could you *not* believe me?"

Later, riding home in Bandeaux's carriage,
both men seem distracted by some riddle.
Though they sit together, they say little.

5

Why, just weeks before the occupation,
did these officers have so much free time,
you may wonder. Were they not preparing?
Life is simple, people complicated.
Months may pass as quickly as an evening;
evenings may encompass years; a lifetime,
whether one in fact or fiction, lingers
within every afternoon of leisure.
I, in hovering above these pages
like a sea bird, may at any moment
veer, or dive and skim across the surface,
or be drawn under and drown. Down, down, down
I continue delving. What's my hurry?

I am rushing toward the tenth of April —
past the days of trouble, past the effort
Lovell made to fortify New Orleans,
past Chalmette, the First Brigade, past Trosler
mustering, recruiting, training, riding,
past his nights, his messages to Bressie
sent through Bandeaux, past her winter mornings
teaching at the orphanage, past her evenings
reading of the war, past Bandeaux's visits,
past the balls at Mardi Gras, past meetings
plotted out clandestinely by Bandeaux
for his "little birds," past masks he had made
by one of his most inventive sculptors
so that Trosler might "encounter" Bressie

without being recognized, past later
when the mayor's announcement banning all masks
from the fear that Northern spies might use them
brought them disappointment, past their good luck
after Trosler left for six-month's duty
without so much as a simple farewell,
late in March, when, due to public outcry
at the growing fear of an invasion
from the gulf, the First Louisiana
was recalled, past Trosler's joyous return.

I could also tell you my own story,
of the rocky steamer trip from New York
to that sandbar called Ship Island. Boredom,
that was war then, boredom and discomfort.
Forty days we lingered on Ship Island.
Forty days we played at being soldiers:
Up at sunrise, roll call and inspection,
breakfast at six-thirty (coffee, gruel),
drills from seven to nine, then from nine-thirty
to eleven, more drills, rest until noon,
dinner (soup, potatoes, hardtack, onions,
maybe carrots), after dinner, meetings
for the officers, the common soldiers
breaking ranks to gather firewood, napping,
smoking seegars, cards, a game of checkers,
drills from three to six, roll call, supper
(saltpork stew with beans, more hardtack, coffee),
followed by the Captains' meetings, roll call
for the General at nine, then night watch,
all fires doused, no smoking, sleep on bedrolls,
five to a tent (once we had tents), silence! —
military blankets, flies, mosquitoes,
stirrings in the groin, vague dreams of glory.

Forty days before we saw New Orleans.
Forty days in spring, the Southern sunshine
broiling our thick, wool shirts and britches,
causing such an itch, as though ten thousand,
nay, ten million tiny tics had burrowed
into each man's hide, the sudden rainstorms
bringing some relief, but with them, flooding,
overflowing sanitary ditches,
muddied bedrolls, drenched skin, dampened fires.
Fifteen thousand miserable soldiers —

infantry, artillery, support troops —
men, all men who sweat, swear, smoke and smell bad,
drilling endlessly, becoming killers.

In those days before the chainraft splintered
in the delta, down below Fort Jackson,
while the rest of us deplored existence,
Trosler came into his blushing honors.
What I want to talk about in this book
isn't of the war — if I can call it
war, not chaos in the name of terror —
how it came to south Louisiana;
wars, no doubt, are all the same, all senseless,
just like slavery.
But Bressie's longing!
Quickly, let's rush on to that, and not give
more than passing thought to sweating armies,
men's unshaven faces, pale and trembling,
swollen with their fathers' pride. War is wretched,
peace more complicated, longing blessed.

6

This is not to say that longing's sacred,
though to hear my poetry about it
you might think so. Think of confidences,
how they're shaken by the breeze of longing
through the trees of ordinary being.
Trosler, for example. What could he want
but to be in love with Bressie, feel her
permeate his fixed routine, a new law
guaranteeing him his independence?
Surely he did not think they would marry,
set up house domestically, breed horses,
entertain their families at Christmas?
War injects extremities of longing
into modest expectations. He thought,
Get me through the day, Lord. This one battle.
Bring me Lincoln's head upon a platter!
I want their humiliation! Nothing
less will do! Just so this skirmish ends soon.
I would love to sleep tonight in silence.

Wanting little from the one he longed for,

Trosler thought of Bressie constantly,
so whatever Bandeaux would suggest,
offered as though taken from the Scriptures,
Trosler gratefully accepted, wholly
bent on seeing all he could of Bressie,
never wholly thinking he would see her
other than by chance, and never, never
(even when at night aroused from sleep
by her body pressing his in his dream)
quite believing they'd end up together.
So what could he lose?

But confidences,
white as cherry blossoms, hold their stillness
only temporarily. A small breeze
(Bandeaux asking him to come one evening
but to tell his sergeant he was elsewhere,
on some secret vigil or inspection) —
just one tiny indiscretion, prompted
by the sting of longing — and the blossoms,
barely shriveled, loosen from their pistils
and in hardly noticeable spirals
start to pull, as though those gentle stirrings
helped them cling to life, their petals stretching
first toward the stem, then in a moment
letting go.

This same course Trosler followed,
not without some trouble, though. In those days,
rarely had he to inform his sergeants
where he was at night. If he was not home,
it would not be viewed conspicuously
half as much as if he were beforehand
to announce his absence, spawning rumors.
Since the time you sleep is your time, no one,
barring an emergency, should question
why you're not in bed. (They might think, **Spot check!**)
So you're sure there's no disloyalty there,
keeping secrets from the ones who trust you:
and one blossom loosens.

Meanwhile Bandeaux,
who had tried with all the good intentions
of a missionary among the heathen
(with about as much success, I might add)

to arrange for Trosler to meet Bressie
privately, had pledged to him that this time
it would happen "*sans problèm, sans scandale.*"
So back to Erato Street went Bandeaux.
This time, though, she wouldn't play the fool.

"What is it you're planning now?" she asked him,
"What surprise?" The winter had been mild
but the war, which everyone had promised
couldn't last the year, had made her weary.

"Darling, how you doubt your uncle hurts me!
I'm an artist, don't forget. Believe me,
there's a symmetry to what I'm doing.
With my keen outsider's eye, I couldn't,
not for all the absinthe in New Orleans,
propagate an ugliness, not I, dear."
Then he tapped his cane against his forehead,
"True, I have a plan, but please, reject it,
any twist, if you find it distasteful.
I've been thinking — *oui, moi* — of your father.
I know how you miss him. For a year now
we've heard nothing from him, not a letter,
not a single word of where he's living,
what he's doing, or when he'll return.
Like a phantom, leaving you twice-widowed,
practically. *Que tragique!*"

"And what's he —
what's my father — got to do with dinner
at your studio? He'd never, you know,
join your 'denizens,' as he would call them.
But, forgive me."

"No, no, don't be sorry.
By all means, be honest. I'm an artist,
don't you know. I thrive on truth and beauty.
Scientists are never fond of artists,
how we chide and twist the laws of nature.
But your father — how little you knew him —
also loved, oh how he loved, good music,
by *artistes*, I mean. Just like your mother.
You remember going to the opera
with him? Well, since now the opera's closed,
I thought, why not find our own musicians?

And my studio is simply perfect
for a rendevous . . . *divertissement* . . .
just for us! And if you like, a few friends."

"For example, Trosler White?" asked Bressie,
turning down both corners of her mouth,
though with eyebrows raised.

"Who? Colonel Trosler?
Well, if you insist, of course."

"Insist? Me?
Isn't it your secret plan to ask him."

"Oh, I'm fond of him, though not exactly
for his taste in music. But if you say,
ask him, I shall ask him." Bandeaux stood,
clicked his heels, saluted.

"Uncle Bandeaux!"

"Don't you uncle me. Besides, I heard that,
what with all that ruckus outside Memphis,
your sweet cavalryman has been sent there.
What makes you think he's in town?"

"He wasn't.
But he's back. I read it in the *Crescent*."

"So, we read the *Daily Crescent*, do we?
Then you must have also seen the notice
that the great George Christy's in New Orleans
with his minstrel band. They're all invited —
Master Leon, Master Bones, the whole crowd.
That's my plan. But now you've ruined it, dear.
I thought I'd surprise you. You're *too* clever."
Lifting one hand to her cheek, he pinched her.
"How you tantalize me." Then he smiled,
innocent as Tantalus himself was.
"Anyway, there's nothing to be scared of.
Let the goosish ones think what they want to.
We'll be having fun!"

Though she said nothing,
Bressie knew he'd managed to evade her

on the Trosler question. She felt helpless
yet excited, when he bent and kissed her.
"Thursday then," he said, as he dismissed her.

7

Thursday came. She slipped her best chemise on,
laced her corset up herself, brushed powder
on her arms and legs (and perfume elsewhere).
Pinning up her hair to suit the fashion,
she put on three petticoats, blue stockings,
a dark blue gown with ruffled, short-sleeved shoulders,
and the brooch and necklace of her mother's.
Then with Alexander as her escort,
she rode to the Quarter in a carriage.
But when she arrived, she found no Trosler.
With her expectations so disjointed,
she was both relieved *and* disappointed.

8

When, near Thibodaux, I first met Bressie,
she reacted similarly, I think,
her distress, her deeper disappointment,
matched only by relief that things had ended.
There was I, a Yankee and a stranger
like a Tereus, who'd come to take her
over land and water to her father.
There was she, beside the railway platform
in her homespun morning gown, her shirtwaist
tightly buttoned, her hair tied back, no bonnet,
scornful hazel eyes half-squinting at me
in the midday brightness. I approached her.
Failing first to introduce myself,
"Are you Bressie LaRouché?" I asked.
She just nodded. Then she sighed.

"It's over,"
later she confessed was what she thought then —
all the suffering, the disappointment,
all the pleasure.

"Shall we, Captain?" she said,

starting off toward the makeshift railcar,
sunbaked, empty, sad.

The crowd at Bandeaux's,
much to her surprise, was small. Just Helen,
nine or ten Confederates, three women
Bressie didn't know, a host of servants,
and Messrs Bones and Leon. Not George Christy.
Nor was supper what she'd planned for: salad,
gumbo, fruit, tomatoes and Madeira,
and those nuts that Bandeaux always favored.
Still, the company she found amusing:
No one talked about the war. The minstrels,
after dinner, sang and danced their famous
"Terpsichorean Représentations"
followed by a "Pas de Fascination."
Next, as Crispus served them more Madeira,
Bandeaux pulled a large book from his shelves,
Tristram and Iseult, a French translation.
First he read a passage where the heroes,
while on board a ship to Cornwall, drink deep
the potion that transforms them into lovers;
then a passage that describes their meeting
underneath a "tristil-tre," in secret.
Bressie noticed that while he read this scene
he kept glancing nervously behind him
as though worried Marc, Iseult's shy husband,
any moment might break through the back door.

When he finished, everyone applauded.
Master Leon raised his fiddle, tapped it
with his bow, and led the congregation
in a rousing chorus of "Sweet Emma."
Then two graycoats started clapping their hands
and began to sing "The Bonnie Blue Flag."
Singing heartily, they threw their arms out,
urging all the others there to join them —
soldiers, civilians, artists, even Negroes —
as the fourteen-foot high walls resounded
with their stamping feet, shaking the gas lamps
so the silhouettes of heads and bodies
formed grotesque shapes, as though they were leaping
from each corner. When the singing died down,
Bandeaux shouted, "*Mes amis!* I love you!
Please, enjoy yourselves! Take more Madeira!

Drink! Drink deep!" And everyone applauded
one more time. They cheered. The minstrels bantered,
mimicking the great Harry Macarthy.
They told stories that made Bressie giggle,
even though she thought them mean, unfeeling:
One about a goose and her drunk master,
how the goose would fetch the drunk at midnight
from the local groggery, in Georgia —
Why must Crackers always live in Georgia? —
how the goose walked straight, the man walked crooked,
tipping over, how the goose approached him,
bit him on the ear, yanked hard and cackled
till the goose-pecked drunkard waddled home.
As he told this story, Leon waddled
after Bones, who crouched and started honking.
Then the entire party started honking,
bleating, mooing, howling, cockadooing
till the room vibrated like a barnyard.

Slowly, one by one, their calls subsided.
Then, by twos or threes, guests began departing,
gathering first to kiss or hug Bandeaux.
But as fortune had it, at that moment
lightning flashed, and then a growl of thunder
rolled across the river, then another.

Helen stepped outside: "My Lord! Let's hurry!
Bye all! Ta ta!" Then she threw her coat on,
latched on to her butler Jacques, and fled.
Others chased behind, shouting at Bandeaux:

"Lovely time!"

"Bye now!"

"Adieu!"

"Ta ta!"

as the darkness swallowed them. By this time,
lightning flashes lit up Dumaine. Bressie,
with each crack of thunder, hesitated.
Then the rains came, gushing forth in torrents.
As she started out into the downpour,
Bressie felt a firm hand on her elbow,
Bandeaux's nails impaling her.

"*Moménṫ*, dear,
Not so fast. No need that you leave quite yet.
You'll get drenched. Why, look at how it's pouring!
Listen to me. Why not spend the night here?
I've an extra room, you know, a private,
very private place. No one will bother . . .
Alexander? He can sleep out back."

"Thank you, Uncle, but I wouldn't dream of —"

"Nonsense! It's no trouble. You're my cousin,
goodness sake. That room is always ready,
kept prepared for unexpected houseguests.
It's right next to mine. I know you'll love it —
dark and private, small yet comfortable.
Once you see it you'll stay here more often,
not just in bad weather —" (here his words lost
to another thunderclap) "My gracious!
Crispus, fill an extra water pitcher.
Miss is staying."

Bressie sighed, "I don't think — "
but the thunder stifled her rebuttal,
rattling the windows, walls and paintings.

Bandeaux motioned Bressie to a chair.
Then he poured them each a glass of brandy.
"There's no need to keep your overcoat on.
Here," he said, "A sip of this will warm you.
I know what is best, dear."

Soon they turned in.
While the shutters swivelled in the wind
and the rain kept falling, Crispus's daughter,
roused from sleep, attended Bressie's toilet.
She undid her gown and pulled her boots off,
then helped her take her three petticoats off,
neatly folding each and storing it
in the highboy. She unlaced her corset,
then watched Bressie unroll both her stockings,
smooth them out and drape them near the basin,
leaving just her silk chemise on. With care
she removed her silver brooch and necklace,
placing them beside her on the bedstand.
Starting to undo her hairpins, Bressie,

noticing the small girl trembling, asked her,
"What's the matter? Did you have a bad dream?"

"No'm."

"Where do you sleep?"

"Nexa Papa,
where my Mama usen."

"Are you cold there?"

"Plenny warm. But I is scared'n dis night
cause dat boogeyman is out der!"

"Is he?
Hurry back to where you're safe, then."

"Yes'm."

Bressie turned the lamp down. In the darkness
she could listen to the storm. Brief flashes
just outside her window lit up branches
thrashing, reaching like ghosts' arms toward her,
bucking in the wind. She heard them scratching,
as though trying to break through. Or was that —
in the next flash — really a ghost? She shivered
and looked outside again: No. With blankets
tucked beneath her chin, she curled and cowered,
hoping the doors and windows in her own house
had been closed and latched. **What use to worry?**
she thought. Slowly she began to nod off.
As the scratching kept on at the window,
in a dream, she saw her father — singing,
drinking wine, and dancing with a waddle
Master Leon's "Pas de Fascination."
So black was his face she hardly knew him.
Also dressed in black, he seemed to fade.
Then he spotted her across the dance floor,
scowled at her, and started dancing, wildly,
so wildly he bored a hole through the floor.
She approached him, and his steps grew louder,
louder, louder, until *crack!* down he dropped
through the hole. When Bressie looked in for him,
she saw only children's faces, all black,

huddled, staring up at her. She fell in.

Then she jerked awake. She heard the scratching,
but not at the window, at the door:
"Let me in. It's me," her uncle whispered.

What on earth is happening? she wondered,
as she shook her dream off. She stepped barefoot
to the highboy where her overcoat was.
Slipping it on, she cracked the door ajar.

"Ssh, don't be alarmed," said Bandeaux, "Quiet!"
squeezing sideways through the door, shutting it,
"We don't want to wake the household. Quick now."
He led Bressie to the bed.

"It's too dark.
Where's the light?" she asked.

"We can't afford it.
Ssh. Lie down," he said. He touched her lips.
Then he nudged her backwards with his hips.

9

Where do you think Trosler was at this time?
Standing sheepishly in Bandeaux's courtyard?
Was that him out there, by the slave's quarters
trying to stay dry beneath the eaves?
Who knows? Maybe he had gone out drinking
to build up his strength for this encounter.
Maybe he had gone to church. One rumor
I heard later, from a rebel's widow,
claimed that Trosler was religious. Maybe.
Maybe he was scratching at the window,
watching Bandeaux put his niece to bed.
Maybe. I imagine he was frightened,
terrified at this clandestine scheme.
Or did he sense he was in a dream?

10

Meanwhile, ninety miles away, downriver

Farragut's ships faced Beauregard's chainraft
prow to link, unflinching in the delta.
Like a school of whales, huge storm clouds gathered
silently above the anchored fleet —
flagships, gunboats, mortar boats, supply ships —
while trapped tight inside their forts on each bank
the Confederates sat, patiently waiting.
In between their checker games, they practiced
at the tasks of soldiering, content
not to have to load and fire their cannons,
nor to have to torch their rafts: A stand-off:
We can't turn them back. But they can't enter.
Both sides saw the storm approaching, wary
of the winds and rain, wary, as dusk fell
on that evening of the tenth of April,
of the havoc spring storms can unleash.
Flagships dropped their sails and tied them. Gunboats,
fearing rust, drew up their chains and covered
with large canvas sheets their guns and mortars.
Meanwhile at the forts, some were preparing
to divert the water, mud and rubble
certain to beseige them, once the rain fell.
Every spring (they knew from their plantations)
all the Mississippi empties itself,
flushing out the ravages of winter
from as far north as St. Louis, or farther:
Melting ice, dead branches, flatboats, fenceposts,
farm equipment, scaffolds from old bridges,
muck eroded from the streets of cities,
bodies of the disinterred, and old clothes
all flow south in one foul swoop each April.
So they scurried to secure to keep dry
all their valuables, from musket powder
to the letters from their wives and mothers,
everything from saltpork, meal and coffee
to tobacco, shoes and water barrels.
Never mind that sludge against the chainraft;
it will hold, at least until this storm's passed.
We'll examine it tomorrow. For now
we've more pressing matters to attend to —
what a soldier has to eat, what leisure,
what his wife reports about the profits
from last winter's sale of crops, distractions
from those ships out there, and a good night's sleep.
We can trust the chainraft; it will keep.

11

Go, slow loris. Take me to the city
where the storm already rages. Maybe
war requires a slow and tense avoidance,
but to the point, please.

Inside came Trosler,
whispering prayers, no doubt, as he entered,
perching himself outside Bandeaux's guest room.
It was pitch dark, with the wind still rattling
in the shutters.

Bandeaux, nudging Bressie,
sat by her, then took up both her shoulders,
asking, "Do you know what state your friend's in,
pining after you? He's like a madman.
When I spoke with him the other morning,
he was raving how he felt abandoned
like a picket who has lost his unit.
Our whole future may depend on Trosler,
yet he's near delirious without you."

"What has happened? I'm confused," said Bressie
in a whisper matching Bandeaux's.

"Listen.
First I told him, 'Bressie's sworn her honor
and devotion. She is yours,' I argued.
Like that: 'She is yours. Why should you doubt her?'
But he answered, 'I can't live on honor.
I can't live on promises alone.
I need something more to hold to, something
more than words.' His words exactly. 'Something
more than words. Some sign, some token.' I said,
'What? You think she's liable to forget you?'
knowing he knows how devoted you are
even to the smallest dandelion.
'No,' he said, 'she'd never hurt my feelings.'
'Well, then,' I said, 'what more can you ask her?'
'I must see her. Yet she puts me off still,
always acting with her proper manners.'"

"Proper manners? What can that mean?" she asked,
breaking through her whisper, "I'm a widow.

What does he expect?"

"My words precisely.
'What do you expect?' I asked. He's desperate.
'Something to hold on to,' he repeated."

"I'll write him tomorrow. I'll remind him
how important he is to the war cause
and to me. How could he ever doubt me?"

"Wait! I haven't finished," Bandeaux went on,
letting her words vanish in the darkness,
"He is here tonight. He's come to see you."

"Trosler? Here now? Why on earth would he come — "
but a crack of thunder made her sit up,
as the wind blew harder still.

"Lie down. Ssh,"
Bandeaux cautioned, as he held her shoulders,
bracing her, then gently easing her down.
"No one knows he's here."

"But what's he doing —"

"Nothing. Waiting. That's why I barged in here.
He's insisting he can wait no longer.
Like a Cyrano, he's mad about you.
In his way, you know, he's so romantic.
You know what I mean. He's not the first one."

"No one's given me so much attention
since I was a girl. But I'm a woman.
Such a boy he is." She paused, then added,
"Tell him there's been some misunderstanding.
We shall meet. Tomorrow. When it suits him.
Tell him."

"All right," Bandeaux said, his long nails
stroking her unraveled hair, "but what if
he refuses?"

"See what you can manage.
Maybe by tomorrow he'll calm down some.
And," she reached up to her right ear, "Take this.

Give him this, this earring, as a token.
Tell him I shall listen to his story."

"Hah! An earring is as close to hearing
as a nutshell to a nut," said Bandeaux,
"Never give a hungry man just nutshells.
I'll do what I can, dear. But I warn you..."
Bandeaux rose and tiptoed through the darkness.

Maybe he's the boogeyman, thought Bressie
as she pressed her head into her pillow.

(Why she trusted Bandeaux, artful Bandeaux,
peeves me. Relatives are so presumptuous.
At the slightest impetus, they move in
as though property were marked by bloodlines.
In a country as unshaped as this one,
property and bloodlines both are sacred.
Once he knew who Bandeaux was to Bressie,
Trosler let him in on things, supposing
that would keep him from oblivion.
But in truth, it's hard to *stop* forgetting
things that matter to you, even lovers!
Once your relatives enter the picture,
be they parents, in-laws, aunts, or children,
be they disapproving or approving,
all that happens after that is sacred,
intimate, and stored in trust, like heirlooms.
We forget; our relatives remember;
and for generations, through our bloodlines,
we're the property of our descendants!)

As she lay there, both her legs curled, dangling
from the bedside, Bressie tried to calm down,
but her mind, in contrast to her body
weighted by a numbness in her hips,
started spinning almost out of control:
What is wrong with all of us? she wondered,
as branches kept scratching at the window,
trying to get in. The thunder had passed
but the rain kept coming. From the hallway,
she heard, she thought, Trosler and her uncle,
not their voices but their body's actions —
dropping boots, a shuffle, someone's elbow
scraping the wall. Was that Trosler stumbling?

Should she rise and find out? No, she couldn't,
not unless she moved this sack, her body,
not until this spinning ceased. She listened
but the branches drowned out all other noise.
So she concentrated on her breathing:
Warm and heavy air inflamed her nostrils.
Still she couldn't budge. Not yet. Not yet. No.
Even her heart seemed to sag to one side.
She wished now she'd gone home, to her own room.
What if her upstairs windows had blown open?
She imagined everything she kept there,
her wash basin, her divan, her mirror,
her two flower vases and her jewel box,
shattering against the walls.

A light tap
and she saw the hunchbacked shade of Bandeaux
reappear. "Bressie," he whispered. She rose,
pivoting upon that sack, her body.
"He won't hear of it," said Bandeaux, "He said
he must see you right away. This evening.
I can't calm him."

"What's so urgent?"

"Don't ask.
Once a building catches fire, it's no good
searching for the broken lantern. Maybe
you can turn this thing around."

"All right, then.
Let me dress." She reached out to the bedstand.

"No," said Bandeaux, "Don't. Don't light that lamp.
Mustn't rouse the household. I'll go get him."

Bressie hesitated. Bandeaux stroked her.
Then his shadow rustled to the doorway.
"Bring a candle back with you," she whispered,
"If we're going to talk here, I must see him.
I insist."

"*Oui, oui, cher*," said the shadow,
slipping through the open door. In no time,
he returned. Another shadow entered.

"Sorry," it said, shoulders drooping.

"Nonsense,"
Bandeaux whispered, fumbling with his matches.
Bressie huddled deep inside her blanket.
"See? That's better. No one is upset now,
are they?" Bandeaux said, though to which person
neither could be sure. He lit the candle.

There beside the bed stood Trosler, barefoot
in his waistcoat, silk shirt and wool trousers,
grinning broadly as a minstrel.

"Perfect!"
Bandeaux put the candle on the mantle.
"Anything else?" he asked, "Are you thirsty?
No, of course not. Is this light enough then?
I wish someone'd stop that branch. It's scratching
like a beggar at the house. Tomorrow
I will cut the tree down. This storm's something!
Never have I seen one blow quite this hard,
one of those strange nights when there's no telling
what the gods are planning, no moon, no stars.
They have left us to ourselves." His head shook.
"Curse that noise. I'll leave you two alone now.
Take your time. Ta ta."

He finally left them.
And again I'm faced with being honest,
rendering what passed between this woman
I made love to, later, and this other,
this strong, handsome one without his boots on.
I've delayed this for a hundred pages,
like a heretic who reads the Bible
looking to undo its holy mysteries:
Might this wine be turned back into water?
Might, just after Christ has cured his blindness,
Bartimaeus go home to his daughters
only to be cast back into darkness?
Why is history so damned determined
we must take it either as the whole truth
or the untruth we know it can not be?
You think, since I'm jealous, I see Trosler
as an inarticulate debaucher,
Bressie as the desperate one. That's not true.

Look at him in semi-darkness, kneeling —
well, not kneeling, really, more like crouching
down on one knee — gazing up at Bressie.
His hair isn't wet but is disheveled
from the rain, his skin is pale yet shining
with the beauty not of an Adonis
but of a Leander, slick from swimming.
And his eyes, those dark eyes which looked through me,
later, with their panther's stare, on Bressie
now, a boy's eyes, filled with a boy's hunger.

"I had no idea you had no idea
I was coming here tonight," he tells her,
"Please forgive me."

Bressie could caress him
just by reaching out her hand; her body,
still unwieldy, starts to stir with life
as she watches the shadows on his waistcoat
lengthen, climbing to his face to rest there
each time he bends forward. He continues:
"I have lost my senses, thinking of you,
thinking how much I want to be near you.
It's as though you know my secret. I don't
have a secret. Yet I think you know it."

Gently pulling her arms from the blanket,
Bressie pulls his face to hers. They kiss.
"I don't know a thing about you," she says,
"but I'm glad that what my uncle told me
isn't true."

"What's that?" he asks, eyes open,
searching for another kiss.

"It's nothing,"
Bressie sighs, "My uncle's so dramatic.
He portrays you as — how should I say it? —
as the hero of a romance — you know,
chivalrous, brave, lovesick." Trosler whitens,
even as he draws back to the shadows.
"No one can go through life as a romance,
not, at least, one anguishing as I do.
Please forgive me. I thought you might try to."

12

Trosler pauses. "Then you don't believe me?
Bandeaux's only trying to be helpful.
I guess it was my mistake to come here.
Why should you be serious? I'm nothing.
I'm one of so many." Then, in adding
something to pique her, he says, "I saw you.
Here, this evening. Dancing with those others.
Why should I get in your way?"

"You're jealous!"
Bressie says out loud, "I can't believe it!
Maybe Bandeaux wasn't so outlandish,"
and she drops her head into her knees
raised beneath the bed clothes, "Trosler, Trosler."
Looking up again, she throws her head back
and her loose hair falls around her shoulders,
as she turns to him, "I once was married.
What makes you think I have lovers? Dancing?
You can hardly call what I did dancing,
wandering a few steps with a soldier
to forget about the war. I'm thirty —
no, I'm thirty-one. I'm not a school girl.
Jealousy? I should pretend I'm flattered.
Once I'd play that game, but all that's passed now.
'And what *if* there's someone else?' I should ask,
testing your allegiance. But there's no one.
I can say this with the confidence
loneliness has given me these last years,
seeing myself in the mirror, older,
childless and widowed. So there's no one,
no one to distract me from devoting
what I am to you. I'm not your dream, though.
I can't be what dreams are made of. See me.
Why is it that you can't see me? See me."

Then she turns her head away from him.
"I could cry. How could I be devoted
to some other, with a life as mine is,
one of waiting, waiting for the future
to release me from a past that's missing?
Who knows why you're thinking what you're thinking?
I can't blame you. But what I can offer
isn't jealousy or love. Just kindness.

Why does kindness seem so formal to you?
Do you know how much I cherish you,
your consideration, how my spirit
lightens when you say a kind word to me?
All I ask is that." Then she falls silent,
burying her head into the bedclothes
as the last year overtakes her, father
in the north, perhaps forever, uncle
blind to politics and war, and this man —
so attractive, so unlikely, so torn —
swept up by his passion for the moment.
She begins to weep, her low voice muted
by the darkness and the scratching branches
outside.

Suddenly a THUD! The house shakes.
Peeking through her closed hands, she sees nothing.
Where is Trosler?

Someone turns the doorknob.
In pops Bandeaux's bobbing head. "What's happened?"

"I don't know." She looks around. "Where is he — "
she begins, but in the half-light Bandeaux,
racing to the bed, reveals where Trosler,
having fainted, lies prone on the floorboards.
"Agh!" She jumps out of the bed.

"What's happened?"
Bandeaux asks again. He kneels to Trosler,
puts his ear against his back, then asks her,
"Have you stopped his heart?" Pause. "No. He's all right,
just a little fainting spell. Here. Help me."

Using all their strength, they slowly lift him
head first to the bed, then pick his feet up,
turning him around. He starts reviving.
Then the sweat pours from his neck and forehead.
"Take that cloth and dip it in the basin,"
Bandeaux orders Bressie. He helps Trosler
sit upright, removes his shirt and waistcoat,
propping pillows under him to rest on.
Bressie takes the dampened cloth and holds it
to his forehead. Then she bathes his face.

"Well, my dear, you must have swept this poor man
off his feet," quips Bandeaux, "Wipe his whole face
and his body. We don't want the fever,
not in this house."

"I am fine," says Trosler,
"Just a little shaken," as he smiles,
now aware of Bressie's fingers on him,
lightly pressing against his chest. He gazes,
sheepishly, up at her, as a broad grin
breaks out underneath his mustache. "Sorry,"
he says. He looks at her naked shoulders.
"We've never been this close."

Bressie blanches,
backing into Bandeaux, who says, "Well, then,
I see you don't need me. Nor this candle.
I'm afraid that too much light will blind you.
Bonne nuit. I'll knock first, if I must find you."

13

Now they are alone again, with Trosler
on the bed this time, and Bressie standing.

"I think I am in a dream," he tells her.

"I can't see you. I can't tell — "

"Please, Bressie.
No more words."

And this she didn't tell me:
Trosler rises from the bed, leans forward,
puts his arm around her waist and pulls her
firmly, as a fisherman his net, in.

First, he brings his head aloft to reach hers,
drawing his pursed lips across her eyebrow,
eyelid, cheekbone, tracing all her features
until, pausing, both let out a sigh now,
aching to begin in on the kisses —
hers for his eyes, his for her throat's hollows,

light and cool to touch, but wet, as mist is —
prelude to that long hard heat that follows
when, as they embrace, he lifts her gown,
parts from her until they're both undressed,
and in a single shadow lays her down,
her hand guiding his mouth to her breast,
his hand on her thigh, which he caresses,
as against her heart his head she presses.
Curling one leg over his, then lifting
both her back and knees, she starts to cry,
eyes closed, head leaned back, mouth open, shifting
from one shoulder to the other, thigh
to stretched thigh, the roots of toes and fingers
clinging to the surface of the bed,
where, before he enters her, he lingers
and, his legs locked into hers, instead
pivots from his hips and grabs her shoulders,
small and round, his arched back long and tight,
bearing into her, as he unfolds her,
forcing both their cries into the night,
two angelic voices penetrating
wind and rain outside, then quickly fading,
trailing through the city, down the river
through the storm, past sugar fields and bayous
to the forts, the ironclads, the schooners,
where, despite the preparations, havoc,
nature's great barbarian, has lowered,
damaging the riggings and the decks,
next unrolling waves in swift succession
southward, broken branches and debris
thrown like cannon balls against the tight chain,
jerked toward one bank, then toward the other,
swallowed into hollows, soon uplifted
as the waves swell to their crests, then splitting
finally, both burst chains rushing downstream
violently, clumps of sludge jammed between them,
as they open, dragging at the anchors
clinging to the sand on both the levees,
and the Mississippi's loot comes charging
through the delta, past the writhing ships
rocking wildly in toylike motion,
toward the far expanse of gulf and ocean.

14

Farragut, at once, would spot the chainraft
split in half, both links unfolding toward him
like two massive, outstretched arms, their wide reach
beckoning his ships to forge between them.
From their posts the guards on either bank
also saw the broken chain, their horror
muted by the steady flow of rain.
Near dawn, once the storm passed, flares shot upward,
small boats rowed out to assess the damage,
and before the fog lifted mid-morning,
crews repaired the break.

But they were too late.
Nature had already sealed their fate.

15

The fog hung over Bandeaux, too, that morning.
He had paced his room for hours, shivering
from the cold. He dared not light a fire,
fearing smoke or noise might waken Crispus,
so he'd draped a quilt around his shoulders
and continued pacing from the basin
to the mantle, back and forth. At six,
scampering like a monk to matins, he rushed
to the guest room door and, tapping lightly,
entered. It was dark still. He saw Trosler
sitting up, his shirt on, next to Bressie,
lying on her side and saying something.
She fell silent. Trosler doubled over.
Then he reached out for his trousers.

"What? What?"
he asked in a hoarse voice, "What do you want?"

"Nothing. But it's dawn. Time to get going."

"Yes. I know."

"Thank God the rain's stopped."

"Has it?"

Bandeaux disappeared.

But they kept talking.
Why should I elaborate the details
from that conversation? They had made love,
more than once, no doubt. And both gave speeches,
or as Bressie said, "made protestations."
Each declared affection for the other:
Trosler spoke of love, Bressie of kindness.
Each honored the other with a small gift —
his, one of her mother's rose-shaped brooches,
delicately lined as nature's own rose,
hers, an extra button from his waistcoat.
Each said things forgotten now, both of them,
in the dim, suspended web of morning
catching them in their nakedness, confessing
truths they didn't know they knew.

We say things,
often, to create the grand illusion
that what's happened isn't all that *un*true
to whatever truth we hold ourselves to.
I've tried faithfully to draw their union,
and I've tried to understand them. Justice,
though, is borne out in the telling only.
We confide to keep from being lonely.

16

There are still more fire, earth, air and water
coming: In a week the balance shifted.
Farragut and Porter broke the chainraft,
rushed upriver under cannon fire,
incapacitated Lovell's "navy"
(what there was of it) and took Fort Jackson.

Porter's heavy gunboats, like large locusts,
sailed into firing range and bombarded both forts
with whatever they had on deck — shrapnel,
shells, grape, cannisters, and burning powder.
Steadily they pounded both forts' gunners,
trying to dishearten them. For three days,
morning, noon and night, they pummeled them,
setting fire to Fort Jackson's barracks,

stirring up small floods, disabling cannons,
decimating arsenals and stockades,
and depriving the Confederates of sleep.
By the third night all the air was shrouded
in a suffocating veil of gunsmoke,
stirred up by a sudden violent windstorm,
as though Mephistopheles had opened,
from below, the gates of hell, the hot sky
void of stars. But Porter ordered more bombs,
doubling them to eighty strikes an hour!
Dazed, exhausted, cowering in their gunstocks,
still the Louisianans held their ground,
praying for God's mercy.

Then, at midnight,
two small gunboats slipped up to the chainraft.
Three men lowered themselves from the first boat,
the *Itasca*, and with hammers and chisels
slowly chipped away the chain at the same spot
where, ten days before, the storm had snapped it.
Both boats, the *Itasca* and the *Pinola*,
nudged up to the chainraft, like two small whales
feeding on a reef. Despite the bombings,
someone noticed them, and soon from both forts
angry batteries sprayed cannon fire
into their direction, sending both boats
crashing up against the chain. The chain snapped,
and again it rushed toward both shorelines
like two long arms beckoning the ocean,
taking with it the ensnared *Itasca*,
battered but still operating. Bright bombs
burst against the hovering black powder
that enclosed the delta in its shroud.
Working loose with help from the *Pinola*,
the *Itasca* turned toward the channel
to advance, but then from one bank upstream
someone set a burning raft adrift
that came rushing downstream in a small blaze
like a comet, chasing the *Itasca*
backwards, toward the flagships' sanctuary.
In that burning raft, Louisiana,
sacrificing itself, made its first stand
as a funerary pyre.

When Lovell,

who'd arrived at dawn, observed the burst chain,
to his sergeant he remarked, "It's over."
Porter's plan had worked, and Lovell knew it,
knew that half the Union Navy, gathered
under Farragut's well-planned direction,
would not long be held off by the two forts
manned by untrained volunteers, exhausted
and dejected from their three-day stand-off.
Lovell's only question was: How much time?
How long could they stall them in the delta?
How long did he have to move his own troops
from New Orleans, ninety miles upriver?
How long to avert catastrophe?
His raw young recruits, their only weapons
hunting rifles they had carried with them
when they had enlisted, now seemed useless.
Lovell's sole remaining task: to spare them,
both civilians and recruits, from carnage
at the hands of Farragut and Porter.
On the boat back to New Orleans, he prayed,
prayed the Federal Army, when the time came,
might treat all of them with kindness.

Kindness.
Bressie's word, too, when she thought of Trosler,
his caresses and his kisses. He, too,
I suspect, in those last tranquil hours,
quietly regarded all around him
with a lover's tolerant demeanor,
tending to his young troops' fears (They *were* young,
some not fifteen!), their fears fed by rumors
Beauregard's chainraft had split. Not weakened
by his newfound passion, nor distracted —
to the contrary, more like an Adam
who, in searching for his spirit's Eden,
bumps into the apple tree and climbs it,
devouring its fruit — Trosler strode the campgrounds
confidently. He knew he loved Bressie;
she loved him. What else could matter? Nothing.
He wished to survive the war, no more.
He had tasted peace and found it sweet.
Turn the page now. This book is complete.

DAVENPORT'S VERSION

BOOK IV

1

Fire comes first, then earth, then air, last water.
All the elements will find their own way:
Fire is heat, earth shelter, air desire,
water spirit. All must be requited
in the end. O sweet Eumenides, please
warm me, hold me, quench my longing, leave me
kindly thought of when I die. I praise you —
mild Megaera, casual Alecto,
indiscriminate Tisiphone —
please grant me grace. Bless this modest effort,
I beseech you, to be fair. I'm trying
simply to remember things — what came next,
what it meant for Bressie to leave Trosler,
what their final nights brought, common gestures
otherwise forgotten. Scared of dying,
ignorant and stubborn, slow, yet learning,
I ask only that you hear me, Furies.
I can promise nothing for your patience,
nothing but these thin lines, liberation
from what burdens me, some passion, sadness,
misdirected patriotism, madness,
infidelities, one night a fire,
earth and air and water and desire.
I would rather wait until tomorrow
to continue, but here is the sorrow.

2

The fire: April 24th upriver
Farragut proceeded with his warships,
taking both banks of the Mississippi.
Meanwhile, we prepared for our invasion.
Ninety thousand, more, Confederate soldiers,
we were told, were waiting in New Orleans.
They outnumbered us by two to one.
Yet with Porter's gunboats, Farragut's mind,

and the leadership of General Butler,
"God is on our side!" they told us. Neatly,
company by company we loaded,
first artillery, then horses, then men,
for the short ride to Fort Jackson. No one
(to our great relief and disappointment),
not a single rebel, not even a dog,
stayed to watch us land. The fort was tomblike —
weapons spiked, stone barricades cracked, barracks
charred and splintered, chopped up into pieces
small enough to use as kindling. Thinking,
"Where's their army? Where's their ninety thousand?
Forty days we've waited for these bastards!"
we played dominoes and chess. More waiting.
Then our first Louisiana sunset:
As I burrowed in my woolen blanket
like a muskrat, a nausea crept through me.
To the west, the sun dropped through the twilight
quickly, streaks of red and orange curdling,
like a bloodshot eye, through the thick haze.
Free from military rigor, we slept
peacefully for two nights. Then came orders.

Here is what I put down in my journal:

Our battalion trudges up the right bank,
scouring the shore for rebels. None there
all the way to Quarantine. Just boredom.
Stabbing at the bushes. When a light breeze
rises from the river, the air smells sweet,
as though, having been cleansed by those spring storms,
it is scheming to seduce us, lure us
gently into dreams. Is this what war is?
Conquering a land by tramping through it?
Carting northern smells to southern climates?
As we walk along in single file,
like wooden ducks at a shooting gallery,
we talk:

"Hey, what are those blossoms?"

"Which ones?"

"Those. The white ones."

"Those? Magnolias, I'd say."

"How would you know?"

"Cause they're white."

"I wonder,
do the women put them in their hair here?"

"Not a chance. I hear they're much too simple.
Rough hands. Big ears. Fat. Their hair's too natty.
Probably have mustaches. Forget it.
It's this wretched sun. It ruins their skin.
No way you'll catch me near one. Manhattan,
that's where women know what every man wants — "

"Are you crazy? New York women bore me
with their foreign languages and perfumes.
All they care about is how good they look
when they go strolling. And their beau's money.
Wait until I meet a Southern lady
who will take me on my own terms, one who
gratefully will leave with me from this place,
godforsaken, smelly. . ."

"Damn mosquitoes!
Bastard draps will eat you up in seconds!"

"Wait! Did you see that?"

"See what?"

"Hey, you there!
Stand up!"

Quickly dropping flat, heads lifted,
we peer through the cattails one stunned young boy
points his musket at. All's still. All's quiet.
No one moves. The soil smells ambrosial.

"Do these graycoats speak English?" he asks me
in a whisper, glancing back, his face red,
musket trembling in his hands.

"I think so,"

I reply, "but I don't think he'll say much,
even if he does."

His clenched jaw tightens,
as he trains his gunsight on the far bank,
till — and this transforms us — from the shallows
a bird five times larger than a pheasant
with a teapot for its lower throat, its brown wings
spreading through the reeds like unfurled pennants,
rises, glides across the river's surface
and begins its slow ascent toward heaven,
lofty and majestic.
"Look! An angel!"
cries the boy, "An angel with huge tippets!"
From the west bank two reports ring out, but
"Don't!" he shouts, "Don't shoot! That there's an angel!"
as the pelican leans toward the south
disappearing from our view, while we watch
stretched out on our stomachs, heads strained upward —
first a shadow on the sun, a white splotch,
then a black speck, then, despite our squinting,
gone. We lift ourselves like sheep, encumbered
by the mammal weight of our own bodies
and our dangling, clangorous equipment.

"Christ!" the voice that hates mosquitoes grumbles,
"Have we nothing better to do than lie here
worshipping the birds? Let's get a move on.
I swear, they'll be marching through Poughkeepsie
before we get to New Orleans."

No one,
fortunately, pays him much attention.
Lazily, we pick up where we left off,
stumbling northward, going through the motions,
stabbing at the thickets, idly chattering,
until, at dusk, tired, dirty, damp,
outside of Quarantine we set up camp.

3

Next day one of Porter's schooners docked there,
tossing ladders to the shore. Ascending
one man at a time, like Noah's monkeys,

we took to the ship. We soon up-anchored,
hugging to the shore so we could search it,
scouting it for rebels. What a fine day!
We, the English sailing down the Nile
or the Portuguese the Amazon,
April turning into May, no rebels
to disturb the peace of our invasion,
Negroes lining up along the levees
dressed in rags, some wearing pressed white linens,
waving, shouting at us in a strange tongue,
while their children, mute, sucked on their fingers.
Was this how Columbus felt on sailing
into Hispaniola? White messiahs?
Here we were, the knights of abolition,
civilizers of the lesser races,
come to make America the free state
she was destined to be. When they'd hail us
we would raise our muskets, shout, or fire
at the sky — to show our holy mission.

Till we reached Chalmette, we saw no white men,
savc for one old man atop his wagon
piled high with canestalks, pulled by two mules.
He would not look at us.

"You! Elijah!"
someone shouted, "Tell us where the rebs are!
What you hiding underneath those sticks there?
Bring the turncoats out, or we'll come get 'em!"
Reaching up to stroke his beard, the old man,
not once turning toward us, shook his head once,
side to side, and pointed to his heart
with his bony finger. Then he pointed
straight ahead. Then at his heart again,
all the while coaxing on his two mules.

"What's he doing?" someone asked.

"It's nothing,"
said an officer, "Some superstition.
Or, perhaps, a signal to alert them,
his militia, if they're hiding near here.
Or he's mad. Look to that shrub there, soldier!"
From our vantage, we found no one hiding;
still the man kept pointing at his own heart,

then ahead, then at his heart again
as his wagon rumbled on beneath him
in a steady ritual of defiance
unbeknown to military science.

4

Lovell's task was not as easy as ours:
first, to save New Orleans; then, his army;
then, their stored provisions, ammunition
and spare parts; and finally, the rail lines
which were now more vital than the river.

First, the city. He had no defense lines
other than those at Chalmette. No pirates
like Lafitte to raid our ships at midnight.
Would civilians have to shed their own blood?
"We can't fight here," Lovell told his colonels,
which included Trosler, "We're retreating."
In one day, at breakneck speed, his troops worked,
packing tents, tools, muskets, rations, blankets,
wood, machinery, spare clothes, live chickens,
and whatever else they could put their hands on,
piling them on confiscated wagons,
jamming rail cars, strapping mules and horses.
Most were sent by train to Brashear City,
some across Lake Pontchartrain to Camp Moore,
while the rest marched west to Baton Rouge.
Then he left the mayor in charge and ordered
all provisions not transported — all sugar,
hay, salt, cotton bales, and army records —
to be burned. "We'll let them take the city,"
Lovell said, "Its buildings, streets and levees
they can have. But let them find them empty,
empty as the hearts of all Orleaners.
Let them have in ashes what their greed craves.
Not all victories are gained through bloodshed."

So when we slipped by their sleeping cannons
on the evening of the 27th,
past Chalmette, we came upon New Orleans
as though sailing into Hell: The levees,
stacked with bales of cotton, burned on both banks,
forming two great walls of red and yellow

that spewed flames like comets through the night sky.
Seven warships, cut loose from their moorings,
masts and spars ablaze like candelabra,
floated aimlessly into the river,
which itself seemed scorched, a bed of lava
or a pool of molten lead. From both banks
men's shrill howls and piercing shrieks from women
burst forth from behind a curtain of fire
in their orgiastic chorus, moaning
for their gods, in their abandonment there
where the white smoke billowed and the flames danced,
alternately blue and red. We watched them,
in between the jagged flames, their faces
radiant and slick, then disappearing
back into the shadows when the blaze rose.
Suddenly a hot gust thrust the flames down,
and their silhouettes, glimpsed on the levee,
heaved fresh bales of cotton on the embers,
their cries heightened, as they watched the flames eat
all they'd cherished in their lives before this,
all they'd worked for, all they'd gladly die for,
all they thought they'd loved — until this moment
when, bedazzled by their own black magic,
they discovered how mistaken they'd been
and how unimaginable this life is
when a people set out to destroy it.
Life? What life is there in things this quickly,
easily annihilated? Cotton?
Look at how it burns, as fast as money
yet without that nauseating crackle,
blue and white flames sweeping across the levee
while its golden threads, like Ariadne's,
map out our escape route. You can have it!
Take our cotton! Hem yourselves in with it!
Weave a golden pall of burning cotton
over your own corpses! Tell the whole world
of its transubstantiation. Tell them!
Cotton! Angel hair! The stuff of Heaven!
Then I thought I heard among their screams,
"Take our cotton! Take our spoiled dreams!"

5

As commander, my concern, so I thought,

was my own dark company. It thrilled us,
those strange incantations from that pyre,
as we stared and listened by the ship's rails.
Faces flushed with heat and fear, eyes glowing,
foreheads slick with sweat, the congregation
at this ghastly worship, we stood silent
until a boy I'd hardly noticed before
fainted, dropping like a ripened fruit.
Then my sergeant drew his pocket Bible
from his knapsack. Rustling through it pages,
he recited:
"God himself be with ye.
Be your God and wipe away all tears.
And there shall be no more death, nor sorrow;
neither shall there be more pain, nor crying;
for all former things have passed away now. . .
I say I shall give to him that's thirsty
from the fountain of life's waters, freely.
He that overcometh shall inherit
all things. And. . ." his voice was getting louder
as he paused and grimaced, eyes turned skyward,
"I shall be his God and he my own son.
But the fearful and the unbelieving,
heretics and murderers, whoremongers,
sorcerers, idolators and liars!
They shall have their part in this lake, burning!
Fire and brimstone! This their second death is."

"Knock that off!" yelled Garrison the Growler
(you remember him, from on the river),
"We don't need none of your catechizing.
One death's plenty for my soul, whoremonger
or not."

"Hell, I'd settle for a whisky,"
said another soldier, "just a whisky.
That's what I am thirsty for."

"If I die,"
moaned his friend, "I damn well want to feel it.
I intend to go down sober."

"Liar.
I'll bet you're the first to find a bottle
once we get ashore."

“We’ll never get there,”
Garrison growled, “Soon we’ll all be dead men,
that’s what we’ll be. Yet all you can think of
is your rotten viscus filled with whisky.
Listen to them! Look at what they’re doing!
Bastards would kill their own wives and mothers
just to keep us from them. Damn the devils!
Think of how they treat the niggers — ”

“Private!”
I said loudly, probably too loudly,
“I doubt we’re in danger here. But keep watch.
You, O’Brien, go astern with Wilson.
Search the shore for muskets. Garrison, you — ”
Suddenly, behind me snapped a sharp *crack!*
as the main mast of an approaching warship,
still in flames, plunged headlong to the water,
cleaving like a sawline through the night sky.
“Hold positions!” That was what I said then,
wondering how soon we’d all be dead men.

6

Just upriver from us, Alexander,
Bressie’s servant, broke into her parlor
shouting, “Dey is here! Da Devils! Missus!
We is got to get out quick!”

The horror.
Sauve qui peut was what she called it later
when we talked about it: “*Sauve qui peut*, yes,
I know what that means now,” she said, “Panic.
How when we are most ourselves we’re nothing.”

Swiftly, after Alexander told her
how the enemy at any moment
would be swarming from their ships, like ravens
come to scavenge, and how they had counted
thousands upon thousands of them, some said
more than thousands, half a million,
Bressie ran upstairs and started packing.
She jammed clothes and jewelry in her hope chest.
Then downstairs the two of them collected,
not once hesitating, Bressie’s silver,

two or three gold trays, her father's banknotes
and whatever valuables they could find
(candlesticks, a paperweight, a brass urn),
all of which they stuffed in burlap rucksacks
better suited for potatoes. "God knows,"
Bressie whispered grimly to her servant,
"if these things will feed us when the time comes
as well as potatoes will," her jaw set
as it was whenever she was angry,
cornered, or disrupted. From the pantry
Alexander grabbed a wicker basket,
filling it with fresh fruit, cheese, beans, cornbread,
and as many bottles of madeira
as fit in it without their bulging out.
Bressie, meanwhile, sought her writing paper
upstairs in her bedroom. In her mirror,
when she glanced at it, she saw her mother,
stricken with her madness. She decided
she had nothing, after all, to tell them,
no words for whomever might come in here
after she was gone. She paused and sat down,
taking two deep breaths, then shut her hope chest
and began to drag it to the foyer.

Twenty minutes later Alexander,
Bressie, and their worldly goods sat waiting
on the levee at Annunciation.
Crowds were gathering at every landing
far enough upriver from the bonfires
to be safe, while riverboats were loading
twice as many passengers as was safe —
groups of children, women, and their servants,
each with his or her own trunk or rucksack.
As though they had practiced this migration
often, they were orderly and quiet,
boarding boats like cattle to the slaughter.

Telling me this, Bressie began crying:
"Like the others, I was hypnotized
by those clouds of smoke above the water
drifting from the fires, by that gold glow
in the distance, glimmering, the stupor
of the panicked families and servants
edging to the landings where the steamers,
one by one, received their lifeless cargo.

Where did we think we were going, David?"
After a pause, she continued. "Naked,
as we loaded on that steamer, naked.
Yet not caring what we seemed to strangers.
Horror tears one's manners off, like clothing.
All was *sauve qui peut*. Yet not a child,
not a single child made a sound — no cries,
no complaining. We were all too frightened,
too ashamed, too numb to take much notice.
Somewhere in our mass imagination
all of us had made this journey, fleeing
from the sanctuary of our houses
into nowhere. . .
                        I remember walking
on what was an ordinary evening
maybe six months earlier, with Helen,
down St. Charles to the Tivoli.
It was breezy, quite cool for October,
and the omnibus approached the circle
where fifteen or twenty people got off
to disperse. But suddenly a breeze stirred,
knocking from the men and several women
their hats — bonnets of every description,
derbies, caps, even scarves! — in all directions.
I held on to mine, but Helen's blew off,
tumbling toward the gutter. She was outraged!
Funny, I remember all this better
than the night we fled New Orleans.
Anyway, I watched the crowd in panic
lunge for hats and bonnets, desperately
like a flock of headless chickens, tripping
over curbstones, arms extended, grasping
at the empty air, as hats continued flying
wildly and free. I started chasing
any hat that blew near me, my body,
Helen's body, all our bodies running
bare, as though the wind had ripped our clothes off,
not our hats alone. And we weren't chasing,
we were dancing! We were marionettes
dangling mindlessly beneath the clouds
which tugged at us with their long strings. I dove
after some poor woman's feathered bonnet
and fell to the ground. My skirts went flying
like an early blossom in a cold wind,
but I wasn't injured. Then with both lips

I pressed lightly on the ground. I kissed it!
No one noticed, I don't think. But after,
after I got up and went to Helen,
after we'd chased down what hats we could
and returned home, I could not but wonder
why I had not looked more closely at them,
all those undressed bodies, dancing, dancing
gloriously beneath that evening sky.
Later, when I saw them on that steamer,
those same bodies, children now, and women,
but still naked strangers, I was thinking,
this is how it is when we're together —
not quite visible, yet not quite nothing.
Were we not together, we'd be nothing
yet together we remain in darkness.
How can we see who we are? I ask you,
how can we see who we are?"

I held her
but I didn't understand her. Furies,
help me. Tear away my hat and clothing.
Tear from me this staid imagination.
Lift my arms and legs and break me, break me.
Memory, stay near and permeate me:
Like the puppeteer, you must create me.
Let me dance with truth, confusion, blindness,
histories, fidelities and kindness.

7

One thing (in that battle he would not fight)
Lovell would not lose was his possession
of the Opelousas Railroad. Deftly,
after his retreat, he had maintained it,
posting guards along the rails from Algiers
all the way to Brashear City. Trosler,
in an effort to recover Bressie,
rode the train back home. He faced no danger
since, for several days, our ships were stranded,
waiting for the city to surrender,
waiting, just as we had on Ship Island,
for our war to start — or end — whichever.
We sat helpless, while the staunch Orleaners,
lacking weapons, leadership and training,

flat refused to let us come ashore:
Butler's giant floating military
idled by these people's brute denial
of our "right" to land, accentuated
by their throwing stones and wielding cudgels
while they threatened us with curses.
Therefore,
Trosler returned to the city safely
and, once he had safeguarded his outfit
salvaging the last of the provisions
for the Louisiana First, he hurried
to Dumaine, where he found Bandeaux packing,
covering his paintings with old blankets,
canvas sheets and burlap.

"Colonel Trosler!"
Bandeaux screeched, "I can't believe you're here still.
Shouldn't you be gone by now?"

"I have been.
Will be. But I must see Bressie first."

"Bressie?" Bandeaux asked. He stared at Trosler
as though Bressie's name meant nothing to him.
Then he smiled. "Don't worry. They won't harm her,
even if they find her. She has money —
well, she has no money. But these paintings,
they're another matter, worth a fortune,
more than the useless Confederate dollar,
so I needed somewhere to seclude them.
Then I thought, *St. Louis Cemetery!*
In Charles's vault, where his wife is buried.
It is empty, dry and insulated!"
Grinning, hunched above a stack of wrapped frames,
Bandeaux twitched and flashed his eyes. "It's perfect,
don't you think? Ingenious."

"Yes, I guess, but . . .,"
Trosler mumbled.

"But, of course," sighed Bandeaux,
stacking one more frame, "It's Bressie you want."
Trosler pleaded to him with his eyes,
bloodshot from exhaustion. With a slight groan,
like the sound a tree makes when it's falling,

Bandeaux propped himself atop his stool,
shoved back to one corner. "Won't you sit down?"

"No," said Trosler, "I am in a hurry."

"Look," said Bandeaux, "Bressie's not in trouble.
I got word this morning. She has left town,
took a boat upriver. Crispus told me.
Why she didn't come here first escapes me.
She has thought of me as her protector
ever since her father left. I figured
all those fires last night on the levee
scared her off. She may have thought she'd lost me.
What a horror! Such complete unreason!
Who cares if they loot and filch our cotton
for themselves? Are they less worthy tailors?
O, I know, I know, they're devils, they are,
and don't think I'll *ever* lift a finger,"
Bandeaux jabbered, lifting several fingers
as he flapped the air, "to help them. *Jamais!*
But to watch the liquor merchants last night
hacking up those kegs! And smashing bottles!
Perfectly good bottles of Madeira!
Burgundy! And port! It's tragic, tragic.
Quel tragique! If they must have their damned war,
why not take it to the fields or forests,
somewhere it won't interfere with people?"

"That's exactly why we left," said Trosler,
"Had it been my choice, we would have stayed here
and attacked them at Chalmette. I trained there.
I know what my men can do." Then leaning
into his tormentor, Trosler added,
"if they'd give us half a chance. But listen . . .
even as I say this I'm astonished
since my words say more than I'm yet feeling:
Where is Bressie? Such bad luck I'm having.
She's been robbed from me like worthless pillage
by a foe who hasn't fired a shot
but against whom I have no defense.
She's the only thing I care about now,
Bandeaux. Never have I felt so wretched."
Trosler seemed to think he'd found the right word.
"Wretched. That's it. I'm the wretch of wretches.
How could she abandon *me*?"

"She hasn't!"
interjected Bandeaux, "Don't be silly."

Trosler, trembling, slumped into a chair.
"I am dead without her, can't you see that?
I'm supposed to travel north. How can I,
knowing nothing of her?"

"You're just tired,
after all that's happened. You may *feel* dead
but that's just the shock from last night's ruckus.
I admit — who ever would have guessed it? —
just as both of you began to sprout wings,
bearing forth your wonderful *arrangement*,
fate would have to interfere. No shock, though,
if you want to know my real opinion.
Think how commonplace it is for lovers,
just as they are starting to enjoy things —
you know, *things*," said Bandeaux, leaning toward him,
pinching Trosler on the cheek, then winking,
"just as things are heating up, to lose them.
Fortune takes away the gifts she's given
yet gives nothing in return. How common!
One may lose his property so quickly,
like those idiots last night, no wonder
Christianity still thrives among us.
But for you it's easy to recover.
Look at me. For me it's not so easy
carting off these paintings to protect them
from those tacky Yankees who will come here
and, if they don't smash them up or burn them,
will abscond with them and no doubt give them
to their ostentatious, frivolous wives
who will hang them in some damp, cold parlor
where the paint will fade and peel. And payment?
I'd be lucky to get half their value,
what without discriminating clients.
Will they pay for quality? Most Yankees,
as you know, have *no* taste whatsoever.
But, concerning Bressie, you don't *own* her
so how can you claim that you have lost her?
She's a person, and now that you've known her,
wholly known her, and you know she loves you,
why can't that suffice? Why, let's be honest.
What's that proverb? 'Better to have loved her

than have lost her first?' It's something like that.
I should think that *I'm* the one abused here
since, though I arranged for you to see her,
I get no embrace, not even a handshake
for my trouble. But, let's not be greedy.
'Just rewards shall follow,' I remind you."

Trosler answered with a frown, "I'm sorry."

Bandeaux reassured him, "We'll survive this.
Why, in no time things will get much better
for the both of us. Don't dwell on Bressie.
She's a nice girl, you don't have to tell me,
but is she worth dying over? Hardly.
This whole country's filled with pretty women.
What is it they say about the fishes?
'If a little fish can't satisfy you,
catch a bigger one.' It's something like that.
Why be so obsessed with her? She's nothing.
Just a pleasant way to spend a few days
in a lifetime. If you liked her brown hair,
think of how much you will love a blonde girl.
If you liked the way she talked, I promise
you will love the way another listens.
Or if she was passive in her loving,
maybe one who's more on top of these things
next time will be better suited for you.
Trust me. I know how to solve your problem.
Of one poison lovebite, I assure you,
one bite from another fly will cure you."

8

Trosler paused, turned red as a tomato,
then exclaimed, "How could you dare suggest that?
I could never, never, love another!"

"Please, don't take it hard," said Bandeaux, "Listen.
'Absence' — what's the saying? — 'makes the heart grow. . .
Larger? Bolder? Colder? More receptive?'
Things take time. But you'll adjust."

"How could you?"

Bandeaux raised his fingers, but he dropped them
once he realized Trosler wouldn't listen.
Trosler gaped at him as at an icon
of a fallen saint. Abruptly, Bandeaux,
jumping from his stool, took up a drawing
and began to wrap it in a blanket.
By chance, it was the same portrait Bandeaux
months before had shown to Trosler: Bressie
at the age of seventeen, her shoulders
bared, with one of those white frilly blouses
drawn around her upper arms and bosom.
Trosler recognized her hazel eyes,
her distinctive jawline and her strong mouth.

"Wait," he said, "Please don't think me ungrateful.
I owe everything to you. And if I . . .,
if I had no feelings, I might listen,
fly to Hell and go down as a traitor.
Certainly I wouldn't be the first to.
But as you yourself said, when I came here
months ago, is it not necessary
I find Bressie and I reassure her
I am her protector? Not to do so,
well. That would be treason. Treason. Treason.
If I thought that loving her was poison
and if I could prove it, I would leave her,
pass our pleasure off as a diversion
from the war. I wouldn't even grieve her.
But your cousin? Bandeaux. You confuse me.
I will never need your cure. I love her
and I'll never, never, love another."

9

Matter, much more matter — stacks of letters,
hills of papers, mountains of court records —
most of which I've read, or rather, climbed through
in an effort to recall this strange love
Trosler had for Bressie. I believe it
and I don't believe it. Men are fickle,
like this weather in Louisiana,
heavy, hard, sublime, but always shifting.
I believe that, after leaving Bandeaux,
Trosler had convinced himself he loved her

this time, and he set about to find her.
And he found her.
Why am I so troubled
writing this part? Why so sad? So empty?

Bandeaux said, "Look, Trosler, I have work here.
Maybe I can help you out tomorrow.
But, if I might offer an opinion,
you're much too distressed. You will not listen
and it seems my argument's to blame here.
If you must chase after Bressie, chase her.
Pull yourself together. Go and find her.
Lock her up, for all I care, and bind her.
Strap her in a cave. But if she loves you,
she'll return. If not, what does it matter?
She is false. Not worth the bed she lies in.
Now, if you'll excuse me — "

But I'm lost here
and despite the mounds of correspondence,
paper ghosts that lurk about my quarters,
Trosler fades from my imagination,
taking with him all his passions, slipping
like the knight in old Sir Gawain's poem
from his castle, deep into the forest.
It's so dark it hardly seems a forest.
I can't see the trees or feel the sunlight.
Gallant, ignorant, insistent, fading —
why can't I imagine him?

"Go find her,"
Bandeaux said.

Yet somehow he persisted,
softening, apparently, toward Bandeaux.
"You are right. She cannot have gone too far.
I will find her," he said, "But to save her,
I must not enslave her. It is *her* choice.
That's exactly why we're fighting, choosing
to protect and save our independence.
When the Yankees took away our freedom,
they entrapped us. Yet by striking back,
we have bound them into doing battle
with a corps they thought we couldn't muster.
Now we're both stuck. But once we defeat them,

we'll restore the right to choose. For Bressie,
who would blame me if I would confine her
for her own good? Not a single person.
Yet to honor her I must respect her.
Let her, like the South, decide her own fate.
Yes," he added, stepping to the door,
"Now I know what we are fighting for."

10

Bressie on the Bayou Teche. To get there
she would disembark at Donaldsonville,
take a packet down the Bayou LaFourche,
cross on foot to catch a carriage westward,
and then ride a small boat up the Teche
north to Centreville. The night she landed
she stayed in a hostelry. They told her
Alexander must sleep in the stable.
The next morning he was gone. He'd left her,
thinking she was safe and he endangered.
(Later he would turn up in New Orleans
serving as a message boy for Butler.
But I'm not yet through with him.)
Like others
who had fled New Orleans for the bayous,
Bressie found herself alone and idle
for a few days. Then there was the housegirl
who, when spotting Bressie in those rushes
growing by the murky Teche, ran breathless
to her mistress, shouting,"Jeesus save me!
I seen Aunt Christina's ghost awalkin'
down da baayou! Talkin' widda cattails.
Lawdy! Save me! She done come t'get me.
I doan wanna die widout no husban'."
Soon it spread through town there was this woman
walking by the Teche, or walking on it,
bringing back the ghost of Aunt Christina.
As a girl, she'd fallen for a dark man
ten years older than herself. She'd loved him
and at night she'd steal off from her parents
to their trysts beside the Teche. He'd take her
on his pirogue through the reeds and cattails
where, concealed from view, they'd coo like two doves.
She had searched the bayou for her lover

ever since he'd left her to go trapping,
never to return. For years, Christina,
not believing that she'd been abandoned,
came each dusk to walk beside the bayou
and, as legend had it, watch the rushes,
waiting for her lover's body to rise
through the algae. Beautiful and headstrong,
she would wander back and forth, her back bent,
arms crossed on her chest, her long hair unbound,
sloshing through the shallows, sometimes wailing,
sometimes cooing to the birds. You'd hear her,
as the sun dipped under the horizon
and the frogs began their evening rituals,
cooing gently for her lover. Later,
when her hair turned gray and she grew fragile,
she would ask the young girls in the village
to assist her search. She died a leper.

Yet Acadiens (this Bressie told me)
still believe Christina's spirit walks there
in the shallows of the bayou — sometimes,
even, walking on the water's surface —
nesting with the herons and the muskrats,
all the while in search of her lost lover.
And if girls don't heed their parents' wishes,
lifting skirts for boys, or falling in love,
Aunt Christina might appear beside them,
late at night, and whisk them through the darkness
to the murky waters of the bayou,
where they'll have to watch for her lost lover,
never to have lovers of their own.
She was beautiful but loved too early,
loved too eagerly, and died a leper.

All the younger girls avoided Bressie
after she was spotted near the bayou.
When she walked through town, she felt a spirit
enter her. "It's so mysterious,"
she explained, "but I felt somehow branded
because I was a woman and alone.
Yet I, too, believed Christina walked there
on the Teche. I sensed her walking with me
in the afternoons. I heard her cooing.
There are ghosts with us we rarely notice."

Two days after Bressie'd first been spotted,
she received an invitation to visit
with three sisters on their large plantation
outside town. It sprawled along the bayou
where she could have all the space she wanted
for her daily meetings with Christina.
Once they had grown sugarcane there. Now, though,
they grew mostly vegetables and melons
for themselves. She gladly took their offer,
spending two more months beside the Teche.
All three sisters' husbands had enlisted
and were fighting somewhere in the north.
Bressie, after several weeks, wrote Bandeaux:

Uncle,
I am safe and hope that you are.
Now I realize I fled much too quickly,
so susceptible, the woman I am,
to the horrisonous force of rumor.
Cities talk too loud, while small towns listen,
so although I leave here soon, I'm grateful,
having walked beside the Teche, for hours
listening to mockingbirds and locusts
with time to listen to my own heart beating
once again, no longer restless, shuffling
back and forth between our streets and houses,
life in solitude and life with Trosler,
neither settled nor quite agitated,
feeling threatened by those awful warships
hovering below the coast — mosquitoes,
you know? Those gargantuan mosquitoes
which form hordes in summer, when it's humid,
so that whether you want rain and floods
to wash out the heat, or you want no rain
to prevent the dampness and the fever,
either way you're left with those mosquitoes.
Once when I was young I dreamt about them
coming in our house and stinging Mother
until she was silent. They scared Father
so much, he jumped through my bedroom window.
Later they abducted me and took me
to some nether region, to a tunnel
(or what I imagined was a tunnel,
never having seen one). I just lay there
on their bed of nails — mosquito stingers —

helpless, praying I'd be spared for Heaven.
It was long ago, but I remember
how defenseless I felt when I woke up.
Here along the Teche I don't feel helpless,
though I'm sometimes lonely.
                                        How is Trosler?
Does he ask about me? If you see him,
tell him I have gone to Brashear City.
I shall have arrived there, at Fort Berwick,
by the time this reaches you. Please write me.
I pray you have not been hurt or captured.

Your devoted cousin, Bressie.

"*Voilà!*"
Bandeaux said aloud, flapping his fingers,
"Soon my two doves will be back together!"
and he fanned himself with Bressie's letter.

11

When I think about my private quarters
in New Orleans, I think how delightful
for a Volunteer they were. I loved them.
After months of camping on Ship Island,
to sleep in a bed again! My own bed!
Caesar could not have been more elated.
What was there? Two tiny rooms, a table,
two chairs, and a bed. With two high windows
and a balcony outside. And shutters
to block out the light and heat of summer.
General Butler kept us busy. Most days
I was out from six a.m. till dark,
running errands, stacking legal papers
(what was left of them), conducting trials
not of Southerners but of our own men
who had gotten drunk and started fighting,
missed watch, or deserted their battalions.
What a thankless task. It was exhausting.

But the nights! So peaceful in my monk's cell
sheltered from the heat, the stench, the madness
of the dirty streets outside. In bed
I'd lie still for hours, barely breathing,

naked on my back, my blood subsiding,
legs splayed, arms relaxed across my stomach,
head set deep into my goosedown pillow.
Eyes closed but not asleep, I'd be dreaming,
dreaming that the sweat that soaked my body
somehow oiled it, making me so fluid
that my spirit slipped out from my skin
and licked it, lightly, licking off its salt,
like a gull that skims across the water
dipping down and lifting small fish from it.
Then my ghost rose from me toward the ceiling,
gazed, dropped down, and lingered by the bedside,
until, requiring flesh, it came back inside
through my pores, the way that smoke from seegars
fills your hair and permeates your clothing
with its fumes you can't see. When I did sleep,
my legs lay as rigid as a mummy's
so that when I woke I couldn't move them;
it was as though they had been entombed there
on a bier, instead of on my mattress,
and were now attached to it, not me.

We don't celebrate enough our stillness,
always praising motion and emotion.
How less human is it just to fill this
extraordinary skin-wrapped ocean
when its storms abate, its surfaces fall
silent, its deep caverns float suspended,
waveless, solid as a pocket crystal?
Was it this perfection we intended
when we dragged ourselves out from our mothers,
letting light corrupt that dark, to rail
at our loss of strength, the strength of others
overwhelming us, all the ways we fail
immanent in our austere design.
Less repose than resolute suggestion,
to lie still approaches the divine —
not as life-in-death but death-in-question.

That's how I felt, my first days in New Orleans,
roving in a daze among the ruins
of its burnt-out commerce — like a goblin
dropped anonymously in a skin suit.
Still, that suit clung to me, white and hairy,
and outside that, wrapped in army flannels,

I learned how to scratch at louse bites, rashes,
groin and armpits, damp with perspiration
whether from the humid air or rain,
who knows? Here the atmosphere's so heavy
it has pressed God's circles close together,
squeezing all things into purgatory,
crowding saints with heretics and sinners,
mites and misanthropes with missionaries.
Angels don't have far to come to fly here,
demons neither, swimming near the surface,
floating up with floods on people's doorsteps
where, like mud, they leave their stain. Temptation?
What's temptation when what lives without you
lives within you, too? There's no division.
Nothing separates the land from water,
what's inside from what's outside your body,
so eventually you learn to waver,
sway uncertainly. Beyond temptation,
we who've grown accustomed to New Orleans
hope, when we die, to remain in Limbo,
rather than abandon it for Heaven.
That's why crypts are built above the ground here
where there's only sanctity and passion,
nothing in between; with nothing lacking,
lying still, or going through the motions,
we drink in the air and exhale oceans;
we are neither devilish nor saintly
but human, and only human faintly.

12

When did I become aware of Bressie?
In my loneliness in my first weeks here,
hovering between the air and water,
I learned twenty thousand names, my own name
often lost among them. On long tables
at the Customs building, stripped and scrubbed clean
like the white slabs in a vault, we laid out
scrolls and scrolls of names of all Orleaners —
crossing off the dead, starring those missing,
and demanding (alphabetically)
that the rest report to us, by schedule.
Anyone who took the oath, we told them,
would retain his property and banknotes.

All he had to do was swear allegiance
to the U.S. Government. The others,
those who chose resistance, could remain here,
but their houses would be confiscated,
their employment cards invalidated,
and, if General Butler signed the order,
they themselves arrested and charged as spies.
Half the city turned to spying that year,
if our rolls were accurate. We'd scold them,
warning them how much they had to lose.
Some would glare at us, then let their eyes drop,
mumble something angry and refuse us,
more like children who refuse their supper
than like spies. We'd let them stew about it,
but except for General Butler, few men,
least of all my office, took reprisals.
We knew why Confederates despised us
and we couldn't blame them. We were careful.

With the blacks it was another matter.
How they'd scamper up the Customs House steps,
gawking awkwardly! They'd poke their heads in,
eyes as white as pullet eggs, and ogle
at the granite walls and columns.
This was Africa to them; for us, though,
with its brute perfection, this was Egypt.

One day I received from Butler's office
names we hadn't yet investigated,
enemies considered dead, or missing.
One name on the list caught my attention:

Last Name: LaRouché First Name: Charles

Occupation: Medicine Dependents:

One, a daughter Citizenship: U.S.

Slaves: Unknown

"Why should this man be missing?"
I inquired at the Commerce Office,
"He's already sworn the oath," a rare thing
in those early days. Who wrote the answer
I cannot be sure, but I received it

scribbled on a separate sheet of paper:

> LaRouché is loyal. Take no action.
> Property should not be confiscated.
> Daughter (listed separately, First District):
> Occupy her house.
>
> Signed, Ben. F. Butler

Then, among a hundred other letters,
everything from weapons inventories
to requests from hospitals for rations
to keep the sick from starving, one more letter.
I can't quote that letter. I don't have it.
It was forwarded to General Butler
and it disappeared, with other papers,
after his dismissal from command.
Strangely, his reply is also missing
from official records — though to read those
you might never know *what* they are saying,
since, as I learned working as a desk clerk,
nothing composed by the military
ever says what it is meant to tell you.
Serving in the army, someone once said,
means obeying your inferiors,
so if you're assigned to keeping records,
you must learn to write the way that they do,
twisting sentences like Turkish nougat
into such distorted shapes your style,
if you ever had one, sugars over
in your reader's palm, melting to syrup.
Truths are camouflaged through your untelling.
You, poor reader, if you're not undone yet,
having endured four books of my untelling,
might bear with me through another season
as I work my backward way to forward:
Bressie meets with Davenport. Both flourish,
as they make love, kindly, with each other.
No one is the wiser. No one triumphs.
Davenport learns what it means to listen,
whether to a woman's pulse, her language,
or the brush of her hair on a pillow —
like the shuffling of a lonely man's shoes
scuttling through the marketplace in winter.

Anyway, pretend this is that letter:

Sir,
I am a native of New Orleans,
well-known in the medical profession.
I count myself first among Orleaners
to condemn the horrors of secession.
How I left New Orleans, in what manner
I fled north and settled in New Haven,
and the ways I've aided abolition
I shall not elaborate on for you.
Yet let me assure and reassure you
I am loyal to your cause for justice.
When I learned that you had freed New Orleans,
I was overjoyed. I sailed home quickly
to reclaim my property and daughter.
But upon arriving, I was dumbstruck
when I was informed my daughter's missing.
She fled on the night of 30 April,
fearing, no doubt, I could not protect her.
She's a widow and she must have panicked.
She is innocent of treason. I know.
I, her father, never should have left her.
I'm the one to blame for being thoughtless,
putting country first and family second.
How she left the city, if she left here
independently or under pressure,
I don't know. I do know she is loyal.
From a cousin, I've learned where she's staying
outside Brashear City. Once she finds out
I am here, she'll want to come back to me.
Yet how can she, if she is imprisoned?
Can you not make some arrangement for her
to return to me by railroad? Surely,
she will come home quietly. A woman
knowing little of the military,
she is not about to spy, and trust me,
she will sever all her ties with rebels,
once I ask her to.
If you arrange this,
she will need an escort, since, as you know,
women traveling alone face danger,
and a well-bred Southerner, she may stir
in some Union volunteers resentment.
I'll be grateful for your help.
Most humbly,
Charles LaRouché, Your Loyal Servant

We said no. But seventeen weeks later
I was sent to escort home "a traitor."

13

Since we are pretending, let's imagine
Lovell's tent at Berwick Bay, his meeting
with his officers, including Trosler,
as they discuss Bressie. Posting orders,
plotting troop locations, signing letters
that requested further reinforcements
for his undertrained Louisianans,
in between a missive sent to Vicksburg
and a field report from General Mouton,
Lovell reads a brief communication
from New Orleans, sent through a liaison.
It suggests a prisoner exchange.
Of the five or six names sent (including
Bressie's nemesis, P. Polyphenos),
most are officers whom Lovell knows,
but while reading out the names requested,
he stops short:
"What's this? They list a woman,
'Bressie LaRouché,'" he says, astonished,
"What is this war coming to, I wonder,
that we're in the trade of swapping women?
What do these crazed Yankees take us for,
savages? No, sir, I won't allow it. . .
'Bressie LaRouché?' That name's familiar — "

"Please, sir," breaks in Deveraux, "if I may, —
as I know about these circumstances —
might I shed some light on your dilemma?"

"What dilemma?" answers Lovell, gravely,
not one prone to raise his voice, "We shall not —
I don't care a wit for circumstances —
shall not consciously exploit this woman,
or, as far as that goes, any woman
as though she were just another weapon.
Have we lost our heads?"

"If I may differ,"
Deveraux replies, "you have confused, sir,

your intention to protect our women
with the circumstances of this one case.
This poor woman's father is a traitor;
now he wants her back. He's not a danger,
I assure you, we must shield her from.
Send her back to him, and in the bargain
we'll receive a man. For us to keep her
is like saving straw to build a house with
when what we require are bricks."

"This one case?
That's not my concern. It's treating women
as though they were nothing more than chattel.
Like the slaves, they're victims of our madness.
Can't we spare them this humiliation
of participating like pack horses
in our barbarous designs? In my view,
if this woman wants to join her father,
let her go to him unharmed. I shall not,
under military order, force her."

"What's possessing you, sir? We have business —
dire, important business — to attend to.
Sir," pleads Deveraux, "please sign this order.
We'll discuss philosophy tomorrow
after we have taken back New Orleans."

"I refuse to sign this kind of order,"
Lovell says. He puts the order down.

Saying, "We will have to take a vote, then,"
General Mouton intervenes, and quickly,
by a show of hands, the rest endorse it,
sealing Bressie's fate. Pale, devastated,
Trosler lets his hand drop, saying nothing,
as the harried officers continue,
almost ghost-like, planning their next move,
Lovell proving what he can't approve.

14

Soon the air, the chilled air of November.
We, the 75th New York, as ordered,
marched our way to western Louisiana

under Brigadier General Godfrey Weitzel.
I remember when he first observed us
at Camp Parapet — amazed us, rather,
by his show of arrogance. He drilled us
up and down the field in slick formation,
double-quick in double columns, two squares,
double columns back again, then two lines
broad enough to bridge the Mississippi,
all in half an hour's time, West Point style,
with the sheer precision of those huge looms
churning dully in the textile mills
in New England. A well-oiled machine,
up and down we marched, those forty long days
we'd spent on Ship Island back to haunt us.
Like a young Ulysses, dark and bearded,
standing with his legs apart, his head high,
barking at us, as though he were Argus
but with eyes that flashed and held stone still,
he repeated, "Left! Right! Left! Right! Left! Right!"
Then, with ease, he mounted his black stallion
and addressed us:
"Listen, volunteers!
By tomorrow you'll be miles from here
sleeping by the bayous. You've heard rumors,
I am sure, of rebel forces out there
fifteen thousand strong. They're meant to scare you,
petrify you into hasty pudding —
most of all you boys who haven't fought yet,
who have, in your sleep, dreamt of the dreadful,
seen the unseen, heard the silence booming.
Listen! I'm a realist, men. And I say —
BUGABOO! You hear me? *BUGABOO!*
I shall *not* be frightened by their tactics.
When I see a thing to do, I do it.
It's that simple. You will see. Tomorrow.
6 a.m., I'll see you at the levee."
He stood in his stirrups and made a fist.
"We shall see what we shall see. Dismissed!"

15

Soon, I promise, the chilled air of November.
But October in Louisiana
is as hot as summer elsewhere. Slowly,

imperceptibly, the bright sun weakens,
and the afternoons, like guests who linger
too long after other guests have left you,
stretch out, their hands raised, crossed behind their necks,
long legs splayed across your floor, their shadows
divulging just how late it is, their warm breath
still ignited from the conversation
that, just moments earlier, had thrilled you
with its white intensity, its hard heat
permeating everything. Still sweating,
still both animated and exhausted
in a kind of stupor — yet now less so —
you observe the sunlight, like guests' eyes, droop
southward, laboring to keep from dropping
off to sleep at twilight. You feel weaker,
thinking, after all that you have suffered
through the summer, **Here at last, they're leaving.**
Even summers in Louisiana,
nine months long, are finally defeated
by the human habit of survival.
You think, **Is there nothing constant? Nothing**
obstinate enough to block my progress
like a Sisyphus uphill? You sweat still,
struggling through midday. Yet when dusk comes
cooler air delivers you. You shiver,
twitch, and stumble from this sultry season
forward, cultivating autumn's reason.

16

It was one such mild October evening,
tucked between the heat and cold, when Trosler,
leaving camp at dusk to carry a message
(so he'd said) from Mouton to the Texans,
strayed off secretly to visit Bressie.
This was not his only visit. Bressie,
after those two months beside the Teche,
had returned from Centreville to Berwick.

"Have you ever felt so *un*inspired,
so entirely suspended," she asked
after I asked how she'd spent her days there
in that boarding house near Brashear City,
"that just passing time becomes sheer torture?"

"Yes," I said, "Before I joined the army.
I was grieving, though. That's how I came here."

"You're a man. You can escape by running.
When," she said, "I thought about my choices,
which, like buzzards, circled all around me,
it seemed easier to dwell in silence
than attempt to run away. I'd walk some,
dressed in black clothes, feeling eighty years old.
Probably I looked that old, too, drifting
from my third floor bedroom to the parlor,
where I'd finger through the pile of letters
posted weeks before, long letters asking
usually for someone not there. Outside
on the front porch hung an old white swing,
rocking gently in the western breezes
coming off the bay. I'd sometimes stand there
mindlessly and press my thighs against it
from behind, to feel it on the back swing
slap against me, slapping me to life
like a newborn. Then I'd stop and lie down,
turning on my side, curled like a baby
in its mother's lap. I'd weigh my choices:
Trosler, if I waited, might come visit.
He knew where I was. But who was Trosler
that I should grow so dependent on him?
He could never say when to expect him,
given that our meetings were clandestine
and he rarely could predict his orders —
Baton Rouge, Des Allemands, or someplace,
any moment. **It's the same old story**,
I thought, **woman waiting for her warrior.**
I considered going home. But should I?
Who knew what awaited me there? Third,
why not leave the war behind, I pondered,
**sell my jewels, sail off somewhere — New Zealand,
Mexico, or Cuba?**

These weren't choices,
I realized, but like scraps and fishheads
gathered for a gumbo, these were meager,
sparse ingredients to make a life of."

"Why not sail back up the Bayou Teche
to your friends in Centreville?" I asked her.

"They were kind. I loved the Teche," she answered,
"but as sweet as they were — spinning stories,
giving life to all the ghosts within me,
and inventing tasks for us to work at —
those three sisters, like expectant mothers,
were so eager for their husbands' coming
(whether on a horse or in a coffin)
I grew weary of them. It was Trosler
they assumed I should be close to, even
(as I told them) it was no use thinking
we two had a future life together.
They would blush with pride as they imagined
touring France or England with their husbands
after the war, or their summer evenings
here at home, spent as leisurely as those
after they were married, with their servants
resting in the shadows of the live oaks,
humming to themselves, the cups of coffee
on the balcony upstairs, and so on —
such domestic bliss. But they were widows,
temporarily or permanently.
I'd been one too long myself to join them.
I no longer thought I could be happy
leaning on some husband's arm. It's something,
something else in nature I seek, something — "
Bressie looked at me across the table,
"something more barbaric, maybe, something
not so merely civilized . . . , but human —
like the thrill of standing in a large crowd
or the satisfaction of a letter
which records precisely one emotion
in the vast collection that surrounds us.
Those seemed to engage me more than husbands
who might love me but might also own me,
or think I owned them. I couldn't stay there,
not and also breathe freely, not live there
knowing I no longer felt quite suited
for that middle way. Along the Teche,
it's true, old ghosts came alive within me,
while in Brashear City I was walking
with the dead. But that, at least, was artless."

"I don't understand," I said.

"With Trosler,"

she went on, as though she hadn't heard me,
"life awoke within me." She blushed, then waited.
Then she smoothed her hand across the linen
which divided us. "But through those long months
I accepted what I knew was absence
in my life. What was it stirred between us?
Love by circumstance of circumstances?
Love of loving? Often in the evenings
I would cry myself to sleep — no reason,
save how little I had cried before that,
no restraints to stop me, now, from sobbing —
and no matter how long I might stay out,
taking in the sun, my body whitened."

"What else?" I asked, after a pause.

"Nothing.
Finally, my father's message. Trosler.
That last night we met. His awful kindness
and my cruelty."

I can't tell you, reader,
what the pain of Bressie's transformation
did. And even had I mastered language
better than I have, it wouldn't matter,
not in this case. Any words I might write,
were they as mellifluous as Milton's
or as sweet as Shakespeare's, could not carry
Bressie's unarticulated sadness.
It's best that I not try, and since I'm poor,
better to return where I was before.

17

Trosler's "awful kindness and my cruelty."
What exactly did she mean? I'll hazard
as I must, I *must*, what she intended.
Without much to build on, I imagine
after she received her father's letter,
Bressie felt compelled to go, but Trosler
(having kept his feelings to himself
while his cousin voiced strong opposition
to this prisoner exchange) fell stricken.
After all, the Southern cause was waning,

he had lost his home, his men were dying
or deserting, and as if he solely
had been picked for Lincoln's retribution,
he was losing Bressie to her father.
Worse still, no one knew!

He thought of praying.
It had worked before. He must see Bressie.
As I mentioned, he'd made prior visits
to her boarding house. But they're forgotten.
They don't serve my ends here.
After supper,
one night, sitting knitting in the parlor
Bressie recognized the sound of Trosler
from the click his boots made on the porch steps.
Alarmed at first, she arose, announcing,
loudly, "I have been expecting you, sir,"
for the benefit of the others nearby
peering out at Trosler from the foyer.

Nodding, twisting up his brow, he answered,
"I believe you will be leaving us. Soon."

That was all, until she led him outside
out of sight, beyond the porch and building,
and they pressed against each other, kissing.
Bressie dropped her head onto his shoulder.
She began to cry, her tears erupting
all at once, like birds that flock from trees
when a sudden noise disturbs them. Trosler,
trembling, held on and kept clutching at her.

"It's my father," Bressie said, "I couldn't,
even if I wanted to, desert him.
Not without an explanation. Could I?"

"Why say that? You know the man's a traitor."

Bressie pulled her head back and her hair fell,
pulling loose her hairpins and cascading
in a sauterne shower to her shoulders.

"I don't mean that," Trosler said, "Not really.
But I . . . , I *do* mean it. If it helps me,
helps me keep you from him. Stay here."

He restrained her. Then she gave in, sighing,
as they put their arms around each other.
What he said next wasn't any better
so she led him inside, upstairs, and he let her.

18

They made love.

But why must I describe that?
I have seen that bedroom. I stopped by there
once, while traveling through Brashear City,
hoping stupidly things might become clear
in the way that solid objects, music,
shadows, or a lingering smell can help you
understand what's fading or abstracted.
What, unfortunately, I do remember —
more than what I looked at in that bedroom
as I pictured Bressie there with Trosler —
is my thinking to myself, **Sad lovers.**
Why should I begrudge them their affection?
Why must I be always scrutinizing?
Bressie's room was smaller than I'd hoped for —
one straight wooden chair, a bed, a basin,
hardly room enough to hang their clothing,
one small window, crossbeams cut at angles
where they held the roof up. **What's it matter,**
Bressie having felt so dead for so long,
she surrendered to his heavy kisses?
What do I care for her other lovers?
What has brought me here? I sat there, thinking,
I've been in the South too long. By my feet,
suddenly from underneath the bed
emerged a kitten, tail held high, purring
as it wrapped its yellow fur around me,
rubbing up against my leg. I stroked it,
lifting it beside me to the pillow.
I began examining my palms
and remembered them on Bressie's shoulders,
how as soft as her skin was, my own hands
touching her felt indistinguishable
from her body. In that room, before me,
had she felt the same with him? How could I,
even had I been a cat and mingled

“Bayou Sunset” by Harold Rudolph, 1871.
Courtesy of New Orleans Museum of Art.

"Battle of Port Hudson on the Mississippi" by Edward E. Arnold, 1864. Courtesy of Louisiana State University Museum of Art.

in between those lovers, as they lay there,
know what they meant to each other? Something
makes us jealous of whatever we can't have.
Quietly, I looked. I smelled. I listened,
as the kitten purred. No moans. No kissing.
Only my heart missing beats and missing.

19

Bressie lay still, with her hand on Trosler,
her head resting on his chest. He held her,
as his body stiffened underneath hers,
steeling itself. Staring at the ceiling
on which shadows from the candlelight
danced a dance of mockery and chaos,
he thought to himself that, come tomorrow,
he would still be Trosler White, a colonel.
Still this woman wouldn't be his wife.
Still they wouldn't have their independence.
Damn this world! he thought, growing even harder
as though someone'd shoved a ramrod in him,
pumping powder into his veins, **Things must change.**
He refocused on the dancing shadows.
I can't see the pattern here. But God does.
If I carefully work through God's pattern,
I am doing His work, and He'll free me
to accomplish what He's always known,
something, in the end, He calls His own.
I must change according to God's knowledge,
yet as true as it may be that I am,
at this moment, pondering God's shadow,
still it would be true, if I arose now
and did something else, God would direct me.
It's not lying here, alone, that matters.
Nor is it true that whatever I do,
by my doing it, proves God's commandment.
Rather, it's my choice, not His insistence,
that reveals the truth of Man's existence.

20

Turning then to Bressie, Trosler kissed her,
this time on her lips.

She isn't trembling,
he thought, **O my God! She isn't breathing!**
Is she dead?
He sprang forth like a slingshot,
then stared down into her face, her eyes closed,
countenance as petrified and lifeless
as Niobe's etched in stone, one tear streak
drying on her cheek. He tried to shake her.
"Bressie? Bressie?" he said, "Can you hear me?"
He sprang from the bed to fetch the candle.
"Dear God, tell me what I've done to kill her!"
He began to pace, with both hands wringing,
tripping over the chair, then the basin,
scratching at his face, banging his forehead
on a crossbeam, praying, "Dear God, help me!"
Then he bent and raised her head. "Forgive me.
Hold fast to your soul till I can join you,
Bressie." He began to sob, his head sunk
in her breasts —
which slowly started to heave.

He thought, **Where's my saber?** and the thought stuck —
like a cough born deep inside your lungs
which, by swallowing, you hope to stifle
but which imperceptibly develops
so the more you struggle to suppress it,
the more it controls you — "Where's my saber?"
Trosler said aloud and shut his eyelids.

"What's the matter? Trosler?" Bressie whispered,
as she lifted her right hand and pressed him
close into her breasts, "What is it?"

"Bressie!"
Like a fish that spots a fly, his head sprung
back from her. "Are you alive?" he asked her.

"I don't know. Are you? What time is it?
Is it late? I guess I must have passed out.
May I get a cup of water?"

"Water?
Bressie, I thought you were — " and he grabbed her.
Then he took her in his arms and kissed her.
She responded this time, and her hips stirred

as he pressed his hand between them.

"Trosler?"
Pulling back from him, she looked up at him
as he flickered in and out of shadow.
"What was that you said just now?"

"I said
I would rather die than live without you."

"Are you mad?" she asked.

"Don't say that, Bressie."

She rose up to kiss him, lightly. "Listen.
I am here for you, no other purpose — "
she insisted, coughing, "Please believe that — "
but she lost her voice.

"I do," said Trosler,
"Why, then, must you leave me?"
Her arms gave way
as her head fell back onto the pillow,
so he kissed her neck. She could do nothing
but let quiet cries escape her.

"Bressie.
You can't leave me. You can't leave me. You can't
leave me," he repeated in a whisper
as he ran his mouth across her forehead,
over one cheek, and down to her shoulder,
"O, how could you even think of leaving?"
Cupping both hands on her breasts, he pleaded,
"You can't leave me. You can't leave me — "

"Stop. Stop,"
Bressie replied, pushing his head back, gently,
"Don't intimidate me. I'm not that strong.
I might only say this once, so listen."

He withdrew and looked at her in silence.

"I just had a thought, an idea, maybe —
Why are women's thoughts taken so lightly? —
Look, there is no reason to feel hopeless

at my leaving, not if we act boldly.
Think of some alternative, some new plan
we can follow, once we're back together.
Help me. Let's not kiss the night away.
If we are determined. . . , please, though. Water."
Bressie coughed.

"I'm sorry. Here," said Trosler.
Righting himself, he reached toward the basin,
searched until he felt a cup, and filled it.
"Drink," he said.

"Don't be impatient," she said,
"Please. My throat is dry."

"'Don't be impatient?'
How can I be *patient*?" He paced the room.
"It's my last night, probably forever,
with you, and 'Don't be impatient,' you say?"

"Here. Sit down. If you would only listen,
you might not be so quick to dismiss me.
Words are all we have." She drank the water.
"I have no choice but to go home, Trosler.
It's a military order. Nothing,
short of death or running off, can change that.
Father's even sent an escort for me.
Here. Sit down."

He sat.

"As soon as I can,
I will try to get away, I promise.
What's a week, ten days, a month? Or longer?
Patience. You must wait as I have waited,
waiting here, not knowing when I'll see you
or if things will change. They always change, though.
If you listen to the talk around here,
we may be at peace, and if that happens,
you'll be free to travel to New Orleans.
It may happen. Maybe you'll convince them,
all those officers, to cease the fighting."

"If it were as simple as you'd have it,"
Trosler interrupted, "I would try to."

"Tell me, why is it so complicated?
Who really desires to fight the Yankees?
Even if you disagree, why kill them?
What will happen when the war is over
and Louisiana returns to normal?
Will my father's patients, friends, and neighbors
never speak to him? Will people shun him?
Who will really bother? In the same way,
even if the war goes on, I'll tell him
why I must return here. He's an old man,
and though he has written nothing to me,
after all he is my father. Either,
once we meet again, he'll listen to me
and together we'll discuss the future,
or, if he will not hear reason, I'll leave,
knowing certainly I've been abandoned.

When I think about New Orleans, I ask
what is there for me, except my father.
Very little. I used to belong there,
but with Northerners controlling it now
I've grown terrified of their reprisals.
I've heard dreadful stories of their army —
rumors, I admit — but there's an ordinance
which prohibits all Confederate colors.
Who knows what may happen if a woman,
by chance, should wear a blue dress in public,
or a red and white one, which some soldier
for some unknown reason disapproves of?
I have even read that if a woman
passing Union soldiers on the banquette
doesn't curtsy, bowing in submission —
How do they put it? — she will be treated
'as a woman of the town found plying
her allotted avocation.' Trosler,
how can you imagine I would even
want to stay there, if it's come to that?
I'm frightened by such strange, sudden changes —
until I understand them. So I must go.
Don't you see? Not understanding something
makes a far worse prison. By my going,
everything with us will have to change. Yes.
But we can't go on indefinitely
waiting. Surely you can understand that."

Silence.

Trosler, it seemed, did believe her.
Smoothing Bressie's blanket with his fingers,
he refused to look at her. "I guess so.
But," he said, "I still don't trust your father."
He stood up and leaned against the bedpost.
You are brave enough to go and face him.
I can't help but love you for that, he thought
and was just about to say, when something,
probably an image of her walking
next to some impetuous Union soldier,
stopped him. Grim-faced, he whirled toward her, and said,
"Too much is at stake for you to leave me.
Who knows where I'll be in ten days. Don't think
you can charm your father. He's too cunning.
Look at how he's cornered you already,
forcing you to go to him, a hostage,
as though you were some purloined possession,
some exotic fur that had been stolen
which he now wants back and so will pay for.
Even Mansfield claimed he is a savage
when we talked about your case. He's trapped you.
I have no more faith that you can fool him
than a man in white can fool the moonlight.
Think of how he left. He never told you
he was running off. He doesn't love you.
And no matter what you say to charm him,
you will not persuade him. He'll see through you.
Never feign a limp before a cripple:
He's the master, you're the imitator.
Never try to out-betray a traitor."

21

Trosler carried on, his temper rising:
"Where do you think you learned all your cunning?
Once he's got you, he will never free you.
He'll bewitch you, fill your heart with falsehoods.
Can't you hear him praising Northerners now?
Soon you will forget what's passed between us
and my weak, unwatered words will wither.
He's a man. You're just a woman." Sighing,
Trosler paused. He'd said all he could manage

to entangle Bressie.

Then he grabbed her.
"Let's run off together!" he implored her,
"You yourself said, when you thought about it,
that's our only choice."

She looked at Trosler.
Then she looked away.

"It's necessary
we act now," he said, "and not surrender."

"Tell me, who did he think he was fooling?"
I snapped, later, when she told me these words,
Trosler's words, verbatim, "What did he mean,
'not surrender'? Did he think I'd take you
as a strategy to win the war?
Did he think he could control your future?"

This time we were in her yard, both seated
on her stone bench. We were drinking absinthe,
and because we'd planned an outing that day,
in her hair she wore her wreath of flowers.
It's best not to speak of other lovers
when you are in bed. You might get angry.
Keep a glass of absinthe in between you,
and a seegar, and a wreath of flowers.

"I am not defending Trosler," Bressie,
after pausing, said to me, "He loved me.
So he was possessive. So what? So what?
He possessed me like a child its mother.
So what?"

"So, what did you want, then?" I asked,
gently, "Did you want to leave or stay?
Really, Bressie? Don't think me unkind, but . . .
but, just, I want to know you."

"What did *I* want?
Two things: Freedom and the pleasure kindness,
dropped like warm rain from the sky, can give —
to behold what life is as you live."

22

Trosler said, "That's it! We'll go to Texas!
I have friends there. And the money needed
to buy land enough to start a horse farm.
I'll take care of you, as I've intended
since I met you. We can leave tomorrow!"

Bressie sighed, as Trosler lay beside her,
whiskers pressed into her cheek. She answered,
"You're a kind man, Trosler, and as you say,
we can steal away, but what will happen
after time goes by? What will sustain us
when we think of now? What of my father
when he learns I'm gone? What of your duty
to your troops, your cavalry? Do you think
anyone would be there to forgive us
this impulsive action, this betrayal?
Should we force ourselves to stay together,
might we not forever doubt ourselves,
our fidelity, our infidelity to . . .,
to . . ., not to each other, but to others?

These four walls, this bedroom, this false prison —
it is not what bars us — nor my father,
nor our secret feelings for each other.
Something — I can't say exactly, but
something larger — keeps me from escaping.
It's almost as though a flood were coming,
covering the whole of Louisiana,
covering the cypresses, the canestalks,
and the cotton fields. It's engulfing us.
You think that by swimming westward through it
we might reach dry land somewhere in Texas.
I don't have that power. And I'm drowning,
drowning in this flood. It's all around us.
Maybe if we hold our breath and keep still
we'll survive a little longer. Maybe.
But I don't see any other way out.
Not for me. Not now. To run to Texas
only means the flood will spread there with us,
and beyond that, west to California.
I can't make the land arise. I'm drowning,
drowning."
Bressie took a breath.

"They need you,"
she continued, "You have always said so,
that you're necessary. Men, not women,
are the fickle ones. You want to flee now,
but at some point you'll decide your duty
lies within the world of men. And then what?
I will lose a lover and a friend."

"That's not true! Don't say that!" he protested,
"I am yours!"

"For how long?" Bressie asked him.

"I can't say forever. That is God's word,
but," he said, "men live for love and honor,
fame and property."

"And women?"

"Women?
Why, the same, of course. Except for women
there are children, too." He hesitated.
"Bressie, are you telling me you won't go?
I must know the truth."

"Not that I *won't* go,
but I *can't* go, not without our knowing
what it is we're leaving. If we're patient — "

"What's there to be patient for?" he broke in,
"I could wait, if only I believed you.
All this talk of drowning. You upset me
so I'll go away."

"You're wrong," she pleaded,
"Can't you understand? I want our freedom."

"Freedom? We're at war! Why talk of freedom
when we are surrounded?"

"Yes. Exactly.
How can you be certain that you love me
in the middle of a war? What freedom,
when we've lost our sense of life, do we have
to express what love is, loss is, pain is,

when our thoughts, our feelings, our words spoken
dwell in exile? If you say you love me,
what's that mean when you can't even see me?
Why is it that you can't see me? See me."
Bressie paused to catch her breath.
"And tell me,
how should I know, if we were to run off,
we weren't imitating Father?"

"Bressie!
How dare you compare us?" Trosler pulled back,
as though she might hit him.

"Aren't we like him,
fleeing that which frightens us? As you say,
if I let him, Father will possess me.
Why do both of you want to possess me?"

"You are mine and I am yours," he answered.
Then he stroked her hair. "I thought you knew that.
We have nothing else to give each other
but ourselves."

"But are we given freely?
Or are we adrift in circumstances?
Whether we believe in love or nothing,
nothing we believe in can be certain,
no more than a ghost behind a curtain."

23

"What's it matter what we think?" asked Trosler,
anger rising in his voice like thunder,
"It is clear that from the time I met you
I was given to you by some power
greater than the sun, or ghosts, or mere words.
I can't prove that. Only time will do that."

Bressie smiled, "That's why I trust you. And, sir,
if I trust you, you must trust me, also.
Think of what we have and what we don't have.
We have nothing we can give each other,
as you say — except our bodies. Here, then.
Take mine. Take it now. But don't possess it

like a gold piece. It will change too quickly,
arms change, eyes change, tongues change, hearts change,
      minds change.
Even as we're making love we're changing
as the sky does during a storm, changing
from a vivid gray to black, the lightning
followed by the cry of rain, the sunlight
coloring a rainbow in the distance.
In the end it may seem right, but no one,
in the middle of a rainstorm, trusts it
absolutely. We can't save the future
any more than we can save the past."
Bressie lifted Trosler's chin with both hands,
as though to balance it.
                                        "I wish, I wish
I could promise you the kind of future
you'd delight in, even for a moment.
I could say — as women often have said —
you're the only world I need. But why,
if by saying so I would deceive you?
We should not say what we can't be sure of.
No. Tomorrow I shall go. My father
and the winter rain await me."
                                                    Pausing,
Bressie rummaged through her clothing. "Take these.
Let me leave with you these few possessions —
bonds, this necklace, jewels — my widow's dowry,
these things you believe to be the reason
Father sent for me. If so, he'll want them
and demand that I return to fetch them.
If not, I'll remind him that I need them.
Maybe you can bring them to me later."

"But what are these few things to a man who,
broken spirited, can only view them
as a legless man his boots and stockings?"

"Never believe what you want to believe
until you can't do otherwise," she told him,
and she pressed him to her thighs. Their shadows
from the early sun outside the window
slowly wrapped their bodies, then unraveled.

But I said I don't want to describe that:
Let their candle burn itself out. Go now.

Turn away from them. Seek refuge elsewhere —
in this floor, this chair, these hands, *this* body.
Feel that summer breeze come through the doorway,
beckoning to you. The door stands open.
Walk through it, and suck the morning breeze in.
Praise this day, unnaturally tender,
cool and bright. Imagine how that other,
at this moment, rises from his lover
in a trance. With quiet hands he dresses,
buttoning his shirt, his thick wool trousers
clipped to their suspenders, each boot gently
eased on, barely fitting over bare feet.
Watch him run his fingers through his black hair,
followed by the quick flick of his mustache,
still pomaded, still awaiting orders.
Sternly, he continues through these motions.
Bressie watches him put on his scabbard,
pull his belt tight and adjust his greatcoat.
Reaching in his pocket, he lifts from it
the polished silver brooch Bressie gave him,
delicately lined as nature's own rose,
and he pins it, underneath his jacket,
to his shirt. He kneels and kisses Bressie
one last time, her hazel eyes now swollen,
flooded pools, and she inside them, drowning.
She gives him the look a child might give
when awakened from a nightmare, crying
yet already nodding off. Departing,
brusquely, he squints at the dawn's sharp, bright glare,
leaving Bressie much as he had sought her,
colorless and various as water.

DAVENPORT'S VERSION

BOOK V

1

Memory is only what we make it.
I invent. I leave you to interpret.
But what matters matters unremembered.
Years ago, when I began this poem
how determined I was to record then
only what's important. What's important,
though, can change, as seasons do, or people.

Take the Freedman's Bureau, for example.
First, the blacks agreed we were important
for their lives and safety. They flowed to us
by the hundreds from the river parishes,
and we fed them, clothed them, legalized them,
housed them, educated them and paid them.
They adored us, claiming us as angels.
But now they think of us as oppressors,
paid by their old masters to police them
taking back their freedom. Now they hate us,
coming to us only when they need us,
when they think they've suffered some injustice
it's our job to solve. Emancipation
means one can undo whatever one wants.

What has changed, then? And who are these Parcae —
Clotho and Lachesis and Atropos —
these dark women some say are controlling
how I tell my tale? In what direction
will it turn? And what important matters
suddenly will I excise?
Resist them.
I'm determined still, by improvising,
to resist the Fates in how I make this.
You decide which way you want to take this:
Trosler's fading, Bressie's disappearing,
I go on, go on, still persevering,
my design still tenuous, still pending,
heart still pumping. Still: Begin my ending.

2

On October 26th, a Sunday,
all day long we marched beside the bayou
south toward LaFourche. For twenty miles
in our boots our regulation blisters
swelled up, bursting into flames like land mines,
as though ants were battling for our feet.
Finally we bivouacked, our first time
sleeping near the enemy, with crickets,
canestalks and mosquitoes as our bedmates.
In the distance, vague artillery blasts
sang us hostile lullabies. The bayou,
flowing placidly beside us, southward,
seemed unusually smooth and tranquil,
like a bridal veil, which we, the next day,
would remove, soon as we crossed the pontoon
Banks had had them tow from Donaldsonville.
No one slept, war's grooms tossing and turning
every time a howitzer was fired.

Drained from our long march, we lay awake,
worried that when the moment we'd awaited
since the day we'd volunteered arrived,
we would freeze or drop our guns, turn our backs,
and before both God and our companions
flee toward the rear: The greenhorn's scurvy.
I have seen men turn and run with hunger,
looking as though they've not seen food for weeks
or — with reasoned looks upon their faces
as though they have carefully considered
whether war is justified and, right then
seeing cannons pointed at their navels,
have decided it is not — start walking,
like a doctor from his laboratory.
Some I've seen, who feel they've done their duty,
who've enlisted for short terms of service,
suddenly decide to take their first leave.
Others, though, don't run away but wander
into the line of fire, hoping, somehow,
rather than to have to lift their muskets
and aim, they might be fired on instead,
thus avoiding that macabre self-knowledge
that torments you once you've killed another.

What is it that makes us so unmanly
we must master death to master ourselves?
I don't know if I have killed another,
but I've wanted to. Was I inspired,
having fixed a rebel in my gunsight,
by the thought that murder leads to freedom?
Might have freedom come had no one fired,
and everyone thrown down his arms? Perhaps not.
But is there no better way to heed them,
one's opponents? Where's the difference? Mired
in war's simple-minded theories, one might
just as well betray one's men as lead them:
No one is exempt from fear, nor tired
of rehearsing how his honest, forthright
enemy might strangle him or bleed him.
Why, *why*, did so many of us follow?
Why did we not disobey our orders?
Why expect death in the name of freedom?

Fighting men require hope to keep them,
hope — despite the overwhelming madness
they are drowning in — that some great purpose
less absurd, less senseless, than the killing
of so many unimportant beings
guides them, hope that someone else knows something
they don't. **Don't think don't think don't**, you hear them
ritually repeating, almost aloud,
as they drift to battle in a crowd.

3

After hardtack, coffee and a seegar
we marched bluntly on, treading the left bank
in the rhythm of Hannibal's elephants
crossing the Alps. Perkins's cavalry,
with the Eighth New Hampshire, walked the right bank
through the canefields. Some got lost and stumbled
westward.
Suddenly they saw some Texans
hidden in the trees. They started firing,
not in sequence as they'd been instructed
but haphazardly. We heard their volleys,
now at least a thousand yards away,
muskets echoing across the bayou.

"Are we going there?" O'Brien asked me,
quivering, his head turned like a turtle's
when it peeks out from its shell.

"We're waiting,"
I said, "It depends on Weitzel's orders."

Then, abruptly, from behind an oak tree
stepped a ghoulish, gray-haired planter, naked
except for a tattered linen nightshirt
and a pair of boots. "Run, boys!" he shouted,
"Turn back while you have a future!"

"Damn you!
Go to hell!" O'Brien, startled, bellowed,
and he started lunging toward the old man
with his bayonet displayed.

"O'Brien!
Stay in rank!" I called, but then my voice cracked
as though I had swallowed a toy whistle
and dislodged it.

"You all right?" asked Wilson.
Someone somewhere started laughing.

"Captain!
That man is a traitor!" yelled O'Brien,
"We should burn his house down! Skin his children!"
In a moment, though, the man retreated
back into the trees, and Weitzel's sergeant,
galloping toward us, brought our orders:
Form two columns, march beside the levee
down to where the Negro troops had cleared it,
and prepare to cross the pontoon bridge.

On the other side, we found our skirmish.
Falling in behind the Eighth New Hampshire,
we marched west with vigorous precision,
like a tiny ship into a tempest.
All of us stuck close together, touching,
taunting, complimenting, joking, swearing.
Then five yards away a mortar shot fell,
blowing two men straight into each other.
One's arm snapped back, like a party streamer,

curling around the other's neck. Both fell.
As the first man's shoulder blurred to crimson,
from the other I heard, "Where's my rifle?"
but before I could reply, a second,
more explosive shot rang out on my right,
not more than six inches from my ear,
deafening me.

"Spread out, men!" I shouted,
but my words seemed lost inside me somewhere,
muffled. I looked to the right in panic.
Then I realized what had scratched my temple —
not their grapeshot but O'Brien's powder
when, instinctively, he'd raised his musket
next to me and fired at the trees
where the cannon shot had come from.

"Spread out!
Guide right!" from inside my head I shouted.

Quickly and efficiently dispersing,
we, the well-drilled New York 75th,
dropped down, crouched, crawled, bellied, ducked and elbowed,
as we crept toward the long, green canestalks
near the forest's edge, where smoke was rising
in enormous white and yellow cloudbursts.
My right cheek was burning, my head pounding
and my mouth filled with the taste of blood.
I tried swallowing, then spit the blood out.
I remember thinking, **Where's my canteen?**
wishing I could sit and take a long draft,
but, regaining self-possession, I looked
out across the field to take its measure,
only to spot our flag-bearer bolting
off toward the south, the wrong direction!
By the rule, I was supposed to shoot him,
rather than let him misguide us.

"Damn you!"
I sang out and stood up, "*This* way! *This* way!"
I charged forward. "West!"

"Yes, sir!" he shouted,
but he circled back toward the trees.
Where's he headed now? I thought, then lost him

when, as though the earth had cracked beneath us,
all at once my entire column stood up
and, in one wave, rushed across the canefield
fifty yards or so. I ran among them
as they swore and called out to each other:

"Cover!"

"Watch that tree!"

"Murder the bastards!"

Shots rang out sporadically — curses,
groans, sharp echoes, blindness from the gunsmoke
lasting sixty seconds (or ten hours),
blackening the mind, numbing the senses.

Where are they, those dogs? I thought, then noticed,
as the smoke thinned out, how close the trees were.
They're just fooling us. I know they're in there.
I could feel the anger swell inside me.
Never had I known such utter hatred —
clean, dark, violent. I felt almost happy,
almost as I've felt next to a woman
I would give myself to, in a minute,
were I not held back by proper manners
or the fear of men's recriminations.
Lust and hate. My body shook. My head soared.

Someone far behind me shouted, "Ceasefire!"
I repeated, "Cease your fire!" from habit,
and the roar died down.

"They fled, God damn them!"
cried O'Brien, sounding disappointed
almost, as he discharged one more shot
which provoked another round of fire,
spreading out like ripples in the water
where a stone drops.

"Cease your fire!" I squealed
just before I blacked out on the field.

4

Trosler took no part at Georgia's Landing.
He was, after his last night with Bressie,
sent to set up camp at Baton Rouge.
Backwards, he was moving, backwards, he felt,
Bressie fading now as morning fog fades.
Would she disappear? Would he forget her,
after he crossed through that web of bayous?
Or would she forget him, once her father —
or some other — wove his lies around her?
What of Bandeaux? Could he be relied on
to protect her from those bats and spiders
who comprised the Union Army?

Backwards,
he thought, riding westward, **always backwards.**
Why did I not run away with Bressie
when I could have? Why did she not let me?

Privately, when he thought on it, Trosler,
more than his own death, feared Bressie's dying
by the casual hand of a Union soldier.
But, he told himself, if they should find out
how he felt, or what his plans for her were,
then they might intentionally kill her
for revenge. He thought he'd best be silent,
hoping that haphazard death stood less chance
than deliberate murder. He told no one
he was suffering for Bressie, no one.

5

Fortunately, no one could mistake me
for the dead. Although I lay with face down
in the mud, I wasn't really wounded —
just a powder burn, and a few thick scratches
from the canestalks I had crawled through. Later
(How much later, I can't say. Ten minutes?
It was still not noon. The sun was shining.
I was soaked in sweat.), O'Brien shook me:
"Sir, are you all right? The general wants you."

"Yes," I mumbled, "Where?" I touched the raw skin

where his musket blast had singed my temple.
Suddenly a flame of pain shot through me
like a devil's courier, a sharp bolt
down my spine and through my knees and elbows.
Every joint screamed, as I slowly stood.
Then I glanced up at the sun and, squinting,
praised it, beckoning its healing power
as a fire that burns a fire, to soothe me.
Pulling out his handkerchief, O'Brien
surgically unfolded it, then doused it
with his cool, stale canteen water. Gently,
like a gardener arranging flowers,
he brushed back my long hair with his fingers
and applied his compress to my forehead.
Then he bathed my neck and face. I thanked him.

"It's a surface wound," he said.

"Where's Weitzel?"
I asked, lifting myself on his forearms.

Pointing to the corner of the canefield
where just moments earlier we'd seen smoke,
he said, "There, sir." I tramped through the mud
to where Weitzel, mounted on his stallion,
was surveying damages. The Rebels,
fleeing through the forest, had abandoned
both their wounded and their dead; their weapons,
on the other hand, they'd dragged off with them.

"Damn! The butternuts have flat retreated,"
Weitzel said as I approached. He leaned down,
as he grasped his saddle horn, and peered in.
After writing down the body count,
without looking at me, he said, "So then,
you're the 75th New York."

"Yes, sir."
(It was not a question.)

"Davenport, then."

"Sir."

"Well done. You stopped them from advancing.

If they don't advance, that means we're gaining.
Go your way and they must go another."

"Sir."

"The damnedest speech I've heard him give yet,"
said O'Brien, when I told it to him,
"Where does one as young as he is learn that?"

"What?" I asked.

"That wisdom."

"Is that wisdom?"

"Must be," said O'Brien, "Have you heard him?
He seems so prophetic when he proclaims,
'A soldier is a soldier is a soldier
whether he lives up to it or doesn't.'"

"What's that mean — 'A soldier is a soldier' —
'We shall see what we shall see?' It's nonsense."

"I'll be damned if I know. Still, I like him,
even if he seems a little crazy."

"Frankly, I doubt he knows more than we do,"
I replied, "but he has what we're lacking."

"What is that, sir?"

"Confidence," I answered.

Following our "victory" that Monday,
we pushed further south along the bayou
from Georgia's Landing into Thibodaux.
We encountered Mouton's men three more times:
After we regrouped, exhilarated,
we resumed our long march down the right bank.
Soon, not far behind us we heard gunfire.

"Center dress!" I ordered, then, "About face!"
As before, but with enhanced conviction,
we advanced toward our rear support troops.

"Bastards are attacking our soup wagons!"
Garrison growled.

"Trust the Eighth New Hampshire,"
I consoled him, but before I finished
we heard musket volleys from our own side,
and no sooner were we running toward them
than we saw gray uniforms dispersing
back into the trees again.

"Ignore them!"
Weitzel called out, as he galloped by us,
"Perkins's cavalry will take care of 'em.
We want Thibodaux!"

Late Tuesday morning,
after one more sleepless night, we faced them,
those whom Mouton hadn't yet directed
to retreat to Berwick Bay. This skirmish —
if you want to call it that — was nothing,
must have lasted less than fifteen minutes,
long enough for Mouton's men to scatter,
scrap, and burn the depot, bridges, sugar,
and supplies they couldn't carry with them,
just a slight diversion from the battle
we would never fight.
In fact, all fighting,
or near-fighting, in Louisiana
seemed to serve this single purpose — merely
to distract us from the one long battle
neither side could ever expect to win
and which, therefore, never would take place.
Skirmishes were hardly more than drills,
exercises in the name of Union
that left most combatants bored, divided,
or, as in the case of one of my men,
dead. I doubt the ones who ambushed our side
really thought they could delay us. Surely,
we outnumbered them by twenty to one.
Still, we lost a nineteen-year-old corporal
from Marmaroneck, whose mother wrote me,
some months later, how he had decided,
though he'd hoped to be a sculptor one day,
he must prove himself. He suffocated
when some grapeshot lodged inside his throat

and he couldn't swallow blood fast enough.
That was Tuesday, 28 October
1862. I can't remember
what his name was anymore nor, even,
what he looked like. But while he was dying
Thibodaux went up in flames.

That evening
we approached the town when for the third time
shots rang out. We had them on the run now,
but as though we were a host of locusts
swarming through the South, they tried to block us
one last time. We lost two, seven wounded.
How businesslike their inefficiency!
Weitzel was enraged. We were exhausted.
But since this was to be our headquarters
he insisted we put out the fires.
Like moths we rushed madly toward the flames,
buckets in our hands, and worked past midnight —
auf zu höherer Begattung, comfort,
by our *neu Verlangen wir gerissen* —
hoping for the sleep we had been missing.

6

How is it that this is Bressie's poem?
From out of the shadows she emerges
now. If I think truth is how one says it,
Bressie thought truth lay in acts of kindness.
Yet, like poetry, most kind acts happen
more by chance than by design.

I saw her
first November first, beside the platform,
waiting for the train, and me, to take her —
take her from her lover to her father,
take her from one prison to another,
take her as she was, and take her nowhere.
When she sighed, "It's over," she was finished,
finished trying to put on the truth
like a new dress she could not fit into.
She would go now naked.

Then she saw me

walking awkwardly toward her, asking,
"Are you Bressie LaRouché?" I'd named her,
as though giving her a name had meaning
in the middle of a burned-out depot
in between a charred field and a river
on an ordinary day in autumn —
as though truth began with Adam saying,
"Eve" to Eve, then "Evil" after — as though,
in fulfilling my role, I was taking
hers away from her. So, hesitating,
willing to give up her name and freedom
both at once, her body and her spirit,
looking like an animal — a rabbit,
maybe, or a grounded bird, its wings clipped —
she half-squinted at me, then asked, "Shall we,
Captain?" And the world rose up between us
in its momentary anguish, truthless,
capable of murder *and* of kindness.

Anything was possible for Bressie.
What was she to do? Her only task now
lay in learning where her freedom might lie —
to imagine what was not and dream it,
not to grow or change, but to be ready
for change, even if not knowing how to.
When she said, "It's over . . . Shall we, Captain?"
she invited me to travel with her
on a journey she would take alone.
Slowly, we climbed to the waiting rail car.
We sat down together. Then the train jerked,
backward first, then forward, when the brakeman
suddenly released the brake, then set it.
As I had been ordered to by Weitzel,
I explained to her where we were going.
Then I reassured her of her safety
in our hands, assuming she was loyal
and would swear the oath for Butler.

"Captain?"
she asked, "If I won't swear? Then what?"

I thought,
She is just like all the others, damn it,
those I'd quarreled with at the Customs House.
"Then we'll seize your property," I told her,

as I'd said to countless others.

"I see."

I went on, "If you want my advice, m'am,
take the oath. Then no one will detain you.
It's a mere formality. The law states . . ."

Then, I *saw* her — for the first time — saw her
as I'd learn I'd always have to see her:
as herself, not as a renegade,
refugee or rib, but as a woman.
Was she listening to me? Was I?
I looked through the window of the rail car
toward the canefields, trying to remember
what to say, or whether to say nothing.
Later (as I've told you) I just chatted,
pointing to the landscape, telling stories
of the hardships of our march, complaining
(not unconscionably) of the weather
and the wretchedness it wreaks on soldiers,
hoping she might somehow hear and take me
for, at least, a friend and fellow sufferer.
She said nothing, yet kept looking at me,
as the *click-clack*, *click-clack* of the rail car
jerked us both, in tandem, to the one side,
then the other, stuttering my efforts
to be kind. The sky was turning grayer,
slowly, as though threatening a rainstorm
later on. But this was in November,
past one's summer wish for violence — cooler,
calmer, clearer. Grateful for the change,
pleased to have this woman's company
yet suspecting she was thinking something
she was not about to tell me, lonely
as a man not used to being homeless
can be lonely, I sensed it would please me
somehow to please her. But how? I wondered.
I began to take an inventory
of my body: what each nerve was saying,
what, if anything, my veins were bidding
through the racket of the train, what message
carried by her energy came toward me.
My hot, scruffy uniform enclosed me
like a Daedalus inside a maze,

as I tracked the caverns through my own limbs,
wondering why this smooth woman mattered,
wondering if I might fly.

I spoke up,
"I was glad, you know, for this assignment."

"Were you?" she replied, "And why?"

"That's easy.
I'm already tired of the fighting,
though it's barely started. It's less trouble
escorting you home to see your father,
finally to do something constructive,
to unite a family. It's tiresome,
always treating you as enemies,
you Louisianans. Not much pleasure,
not in that, for me. I'd rather help you,
though I guess you think me more a problem
than an answer. Not that you're the victims.
By your own decisions you deserve this — "
and I gestured to the open window
where the broad expanse of fields passed by us,
"Anyone who flaunts his wealth from thieving,
who strips bare the land and laborers both
for his own preferment, can't be pitied
when the odds catch up to him. It's his fault.
But I dread how we, too, might destroy this,
all this fertile land, and will exploit them,
all your Negroes, drenched in your own image.
I'm no farmer, but it won't surprise me,
after all the trooping we've done through them,
if these canefields never produce again.
I'd prefer to make things better, not worse —
or, at least, bring families together."

Much as I believed what I had told her,
in the saying of it, it seemed facile,
sentimental. Yet, not one to drop out
once I've started something, I plunged forward:
One who never takes a risk is foolish.

"Listen," I said, "Probably I can't help,
but I wonder . . ., maybe, might you trust me?
I don't have a friend within a thousand,

nay, two thousand miles. Lord knows I need one.
You look, too, as though you could afford one — ”

And she did! She did! Her hair was scraggly,
falling from her ears where she had tucked it,
and her face looked tired, a glaze across it,
eyes green from the afternoon's cloud cover,
lips uneven, forehead wrinkled slightly,
hollowed cheeks, red nostrils, eyelids swollen.
What she had been once no longer suited
yet what she was now was changing, changing
there before me — like those Chinese flowers
which unfold their petals in one motion
when you drop them in a glass of water.
She was shedding something which had hurt her.
This I saw. Still I longed to say one thing:
She was beautiful. Not like some violet
unattended in a morning garden
but more like a willow tree at midday
looked on from a distance: drooping, breezy,
place for shade and comfort.
I stopped talking,
having grown impatient with her silence
and embarrassed by my own arrogance:
What are we but passengers together?
I thought, **No need to oblige her. Leave her.**
Two more hours to the Algiers Depot.
Ah! This evening I'll be in New Orleans.
Home again!
I thought about my freedom,
almost tasting it, as out the window
canefield after canefield passed beside us.
I thought of my lodgings, Royal Street,
spicey smells from Quarter restaurants,
women white with parasols, pink dresses,
banjo music rising from the side streets,
black men selling vegetables, mosquitoes,
kerosene lamps, carriages and wagons
rumbling by my balcony at midnight,
laughter from below, as small crowds wandered
from one unknown party to another,
whisky, seegars, quiet Sunday mornings,
breezes off the river, fresh bread, coffee.
I must have decided at that moment
that, if I did not die, I would stay on

in New Orleans, when the war was over.
Writing this, I realize it was Bressie,
sitting there across from me — gray, hopeless,
elegant, disarming — who first stirred me
for this city I had come to cherish.

Obviously sad, but steady, she gazed
straight ahead: I knew she hadn't listened
more than to a word or two I'd spoken.
What was I to her? A ghost. An escort.
Yet not since New York had I felt this clear.

"I love New Orleans," I said, in a whisper.

Then she answered: "I don't know who I am.
Have you ever felt that way? It's puzzling,
not particularly bad, not knowing.
Once I thought I knew just how to be
and how not to be. But now I can't tell.
What am I supposed to say to someone,
someone such as you, sir? I feel foolish,
saying nothing. But whatever I think,
saying it seems wrong, as though my language,
which for years has been as loyal to me
as a sister or a son, has left me,
forcing me once more to start things over."
She looked straight at me — and I at her.
"What's your name? Your real name?"

"David," I said,
blushing like a child before his classmates.

Then I cleared my throat and said, "I'm thirsty.
Are you thirsty? I am. I have water.
In my canteen. Over there." I pointed
by her shoulder at my knapsack.

"David,
water would be just the thing." She smiled.
I was taken, mesmerized, beguiled.

7

As we slowed and neared the depot, Bressie,
having had a long drink from my canteen,
gazed out on the river, now approaching,
opening before us in a crescent.
She fell back against her seat, her forehead
leaning on the window frame. Was Trosler
whom she thought of then? I left her silent,
rose, and walked to one end of the rail car
where I gathered up her luggage.
Jerked
forward, as the brakeman put the brake on,
we came to a dead halt. Then the noise died,
bringing on a blessed stillness. Sunlight,
streaming suddenly through every window,
lit up Bressie's body, while I watched her
from behind, her hair shone yellow, shoulders
leaning to one side. She let her head drop,
as she looked out on the small crowd gathered
at the depot, searching for her father.
I looked out and guessed at once which he was,
in his long, black overcoat and top hat,
with his round face grinning through his mustache,
paler skin than hers, his tailored shoulders
and his stately build — the lone civilian
on the platform, bouncing up and down
to catch a glimpse of her through the windows,
nervous, happy, full of self-importance,
as though Bressie were returning to him
from a lengthy holiday in Europe.
I approached her, "Let me take your things — "

"No,
you have been . . . , it's . . . , I'm fine, David . . . , really,
thank you." She kept glancing out the window.

I put down her bags. "It's nothing, nothing.
I hope you will contact me if you need . . . "
I, too, looked outside, "And, well, I'd like to . . . ,
I mean, might I call on you?"

"I'd like that,
sometime," with civility she answered,
and she told me where her father lived.

Then she rose, extending both arms toward me.

"Well, then. Soon," I said and took her gently
by her elbows.

"May I have my bags, please?
I can carry them," she said.

Embarrassed,
I let go of her and whisked her bags off
gingerly toward the door. "I'll take them.
Let me take them to the ferry landing,"
but no sooner had I stepped down with them
then I saw the two of them embracing.
Twenty times he must have kissed her, crying,
each time drawing back to gaze down on her,
then enfolding her again.

"Dear daughter!
Welcome home!" he cried, "My dear, dear Bressie!"

"I'm so glad to see you, Father," she said,
not so loudly, as he started sobbing.

"How long has it been? O, how I've missed you!
I don't know how I could ever leave you.
Bressie mine!"

I tottered to the ferry,
legs still wobbly from the ride, heart weary.

8

I have several letters here from Trosler
to his "dear friend" Bandeaux, sent covertly
from his post in Baton Rouge. They're too long
to quote all their contents; he writes, mostly,
things he otherwise kept to himself:
his despair at being far from "That One,"
herself "in the clutches of those buzzards,"
how, since she had gone, the days seemed endless,
all four of them, phrases such as "Curse me!"
"Curse the sun!" "Curse nature!" reappearing
in each letter, separately but scattered,

as though he had written all at one time
but had sent them by assorted couriers,
multiplying the odds — the same technique used
to convey war secrets past the sentries
by barraging them with so much detail,
or what looks like detail, they grow weary
and believe it's all a hoax. Who knows, then,
how much weight he really lost "in mourning,"
or how serious he was when he wrote
he would "drain" his own "blood" ten days "from now"
if his "ally" didn't come and "claim" him.

Then he writes about his dreams, in these terms:

> Last night I awoke from one dream sweating,
> knowing I shall not survive. My brain's cursed.
> I went back to sleep and dreamt of battles.
> Bluecoats everywhere around me, pointing
> guns and bayonets straight at my white heart.
> They crept closer. Suddenly I crumpled,
> falling into That One's arms. Her eyes burned.
> I was bloody as a corpse, my hands gone,
> severed at the wrists. I woke up sweating,
> drenched in sweat, not blood. But it was *real! Real!*
> *I dreamt of my death in her arms!*

Like this
he goes on for one or two more pages,
agonizing. There was something to it,
I admit, his sheer devotion to her,
whether it was her or just her image.
But love is not for me to measure. Not here.
But I'm weary of him.

Then, I've since learned,
three days after Trosler's letters reached him,
Bandeaux did in fact go visit Trosler.
First he took a skiff to Burnside Mansion
to conduct some business. Two days later
he reached Baton Rouge, where he found Trosler
in his private tent, alone and sickly,
stretched out on his cot.

"I'd been here sooner,"
Bandeaux burst out as he walked in, breathless,

"but for this small matter of a painting,
quite a lovely one, a woman's portrait
in the manner of a Botticelli,
beautiful as Venus, by Paul Poincy,
for which I have found a gracious buyer.
Seven hundred Irish dollars! *Bonne chance!*
I could not delay a single hour . . . "
Bandeaux dropped his coat on Trosler's field desk,
neatly folding it first. "There now. So then,
how's our patient? From your letters I'd say
not so well, not well at all."

And Trosler,
looking pale as a chameleon, said,
"It's not fever. Still, I can't keep food down.
It's this muddy camp. But tell me . . . Bressie . . . "
(For a week he hadn't voiced her name.)

"As I've told you, I've not had a minute.
She stays with her father. Listen, *mon frère*,"
Bandeaux sighed and sat down next to Trosler,
"she'll return to you. You're not the first man
to be separated from his mistress."

Trosler winced, not liking Bandeaux's word choice.
"Well," he answered, "you, at least, are here now.
If I die, I — "

Bandeaux raised his left hand,
silencing the tent, then placed the same hand
inside Trosler's knee. "Don't talk such nonsense.
I shall not allow this. It's been six days,
seven at the most. Why, every sane man,
when it's necessary, leaves his woman
for a month or season at a time.
Yet he'll swear there's nothing more important
than her and her health. You're still a young man — "

"Let me finish. I know what you're thinking.
I don't want to die, but when it happens,
I wish to be cremated, my ashes
placed inside a golden urn for keeping —
one's available, I've paid the small fee
to reserve it. Give that urn to Bressie.
I have written down your name. Please take this.

Tell me that the dust my heart once beat in
will be hers forever."

"Will you stop this!
Too too morbid!" Bandeaux interjected,
brushing dust from his lapel, "I tell you
I have not tramped all this way to hear you
sing some swan song. Can't we change the subject?"

"Such extraordinary dreams I'm having.
I wrote you about them. With that owl
devouring me as though I were a mouse.
If I die soon — "

"Let me tell you something,"
Bandeaux broke in, "No one buys that dream talk
anymore. Back in the Darker Ages
people believed dreams foretold disaster
and that God communicated with them
in their sleep. Who was that Spanish painter —
you know, that Greek? He knew all about that.
But have not you heard? We have progressed, friend.
Now they say nightmares come from what you eat
or, as you've admitted, what you *don't* eat.
Doctors recommend hot milk and brandy,
that's the antidote. At one time leeches —
probably you're too young to remember —
used to be applied to suck the blood out
and restore one's balance. But in those days
dreamers often were considered madmen.
We know better now: You have desires
you're not acting on. Instead, you dream them
in unrecognizable shapes — owls, say.
Owls have nothing whatsoever to do with
what occurs when you're awake. Your future,
Bressie's, too, is as secure as mine is.
Rather than fear dreams, you should act on them,
use that manly energy of yours
elsewhere. It's *furor fugere*, I think,
some such scientific name. My poor boy,
you should take the time to read more often
so you don't miss out on these advancements.
How our world is changing! Like a sunset
every moment brilliant colors glowing . . . "

"Then the darkness," Trosler muttered.

"Pardon?"

Bandeaux had not heard him, or thought better
than to listen. "Yes. That's it! A brandy!
Pack away your silly superstitions.
You're not really that ill. If you stay here,
others may become suspicious. Listen.
There's a place a mile or so down river —
Sarpedon's, it's called — a little tavern
by the levee, which I saw in passing.
Out of bed, T.B.! Put on your jacket.
I have made a sale. Let's celebrate it.
I believe he keeps some dancing girls there,"
Bandeaux leaned across the cot, "Fine ladies
lonely for fine gentlemen?" He simpered.
"Won't you come along? Before you know it,
Bressie will return to you. Until then
why not fill your days in search of heaven
here on earth? *Allons!* Up on your feet, sir!
Trust me. Dancing helps one's dreams turn sweeter."

9

I imagine this:

Beside the levee
stands a cypress tavern, two stories high.
Downstairs are a twenty-five foot bar rail
(also made of cypress), fifteen tables
pushed aside to shape a dance floor, lanterns
hanging from the rafters, and young women
who have come from who knows where, their dresses
pressed from cotton dyed in reds and yellows,
some in high-topped buttoned shoes, some barefoot,
thick hair tied with ribbons or pinned up,
Sarpedon at one end with his fiddle
(which he bought, or stole, in Alexandria)
playing French or old Greek ballads, soldiers,
officers and volunteers together,
passing bottles back and forth, some gulping
with defiant gestures, some smacking lips,
grabbing girls to dance or go upstairs with,
some just sitting, joking with each other,
putting arms on one another's shoulders,

swearing drunken oaths of their allegiance
to the South.

Old Sarpedon (who later
at the hands of one of Butler's majors
lost his life in a duel) was over sixty.
Some said he was eighty-five or older.
He was Greek but sided with the Rebels,
given his long friendship with John Burnside
who owned half the slaves in St. James Parish.
Sarpey, mostly, loved large crowds. His parties,
sometimes, lasted several days. And this time
with the Yankees fast approaching, no one,
not old Sarpedon, not even Lovell,
thought it would be long before the state fell.
This time he intended to bring pleasure
for at least a week to every soldier
who should happen by.

So in walks Trosler
who, once he observes the revelry here,
wishes he had stayed behind. "What is this?"
he asks.

"Welcome to New Sarpy's Tavern.
Here. Sit down," says Bandeaux, "Take your coat off,"
as he chauffeurs Trosler to a table.
"First, a milk and brandy. That's what you need."

Trosler scans the room. He spots a woman,
brown-haired, wearing ruffled skirts and pink lace,
at a corner table. She is laughing
as she drops her head onto the shoulder
of the colonel next to her, who chuckles,
takes a long draw from his seegar, goes on
joking with his fellow officers,
meanwhile latching one arm to the woman.
She leans back, her eyes closed. Then her head turns,
faintly, as though she can feel a presence,
and she winks at Trosler. **She's not Bressie**,
he thinks, but his eyes see only Bressie.
He avoids her look. "What is wrong with me?"
he asks himself aloud.

"Never mind that,"

Bandeaux answers, returning with two cups,
"I guess you don't like Old Sarpy's music.
That's his way. The man's a saint — here, drink this —
taking in these poor folk."

After three cups,
Bandeaux switches from the milk and brandy
to Madeira. Trosler starts relaxing.
"Never have I seen so many beauties
in a single place," he drawls out, slowly,
"Ne-ver. Beau-ties. Sin-gle."

"Now you're talking!"
Bandeaux chirps. He puts his arm around him,
"Tell me, which one suits your fancy?" Sarpy,
joined here by a man who plays piano,
breaks into an Irish jig. The dance floor,
largely empty up to now, starts filling.

"Well, now," Trosler squints to stop the blurring.
He surveys the room. A girl with plump cheeks,
white as clouds, her red lips smiling, dances
only half a yard away. His mouth drops.
She's not yet sixteen. The others near her,
bodies ripe to pluck, seem even younger.
"None do."

"None do?"

"On-ly Bres-sie suit-sme."
Trosler takes a long drink from his wine cup,
as bodies flood the red behind his closed eyes.
When he opens them, he sees a woman
dressed in black, her hair in curls, her back turned
as she dances with a tall, thin soldier.
Drunk, he waits for her to shift. His eyes run
from her bouncing feet, long skirt and thin waist
up her back and shoulders to her bare neck.
Something stirs in him. But then he sees him,
that familiar face she's dancing with —
Deveraux, now locked in her embrace!
"Uh,"
Trosler slurs and starts to rise, "Uh'm lee-ving."

"Wait!" cries Bandeaux, "Don't go, what's the — Colonel!"

Trosler's out the door now, in the twilight,
stumbling up the levee toward the river.
Bandeaux stumbles after. "We can't leave now."

"That would be much better than to catch her.
Catch her everywhere betraying our love."

"Slow down, will you?" Bandeaux pleads, "You're climbing
much too fast, and God knows what is slinking
through these grasses." Trosler grabs his elbow,
almost lifting Bandeaux to the levee.
In the growing dark, they watch the river
shimmering in silence.

Trosler whispers,
"Some-where down there Bres-sie's eating supper.
Drinking tea. Or putting on her night-gown.
But without me."

"What's the matter with you?
Sarpedon invited us. To leave now —
it would be discourteous. Believe me,
Bressie will return, and when she does come,
you will long for these days, for your freedom."

"Free-dom? Who wants free-dom," Trosler answers,
"when he might have Bres-sie?"

"*You* will. You'll see."

Trosler looks up at the sky. "Be-lieve you?
All I've ever done is just believe you.
Now look at me. I'm more mis-er-a-ble
than I've ever been. Why have you fooled me?
You, who've known her all her life, protect her
as though she were one of your, your pain-tings.
She is not. She's flesh, she's blood. A wo-man.
And just like her father she'll betray me.
All the pieces of the world are fly-ing,
loosed from their moorings. Like stars. There's your free-dom."
He begins to sway and flap his arms,
head turned upward. Then he drops to his knees.
"You can have your free-dom. I want Bres-sie."

Bandeaux thinks, **He should have skipped that last cup.**

"Listen. You're not well," he whispers, "Come now.
It's too cold out here to stay much longer,
and I wonder what our friends are up to.
Let's inside."
                He slips his arms around him,
gently lifting Trosler to his feet.
Soon they pick their way back through the grasses.
Trosler has another drink. Time passes.

10

Back to Bressie, nine days after leaving.
During this time she stayed with her father.
Only twice did she go to Erato
to inspect her house and its belongings,
what was left of them. It had been claimed now
by five officers to be their barracks.
Since she'd left by choice, she had no rights,
not until she swore the oath. And after,
still there'd be delays. The bayou campaign,
now well under way, had slowed our efforts
to administer civilian matters.

Killing rebels had become more urgent
than the supervision of survivors.
Butler ran New Orleans as it pleased him,
rarely bothering with details — Bressie,
for example. Since her house was useful
and the paperwork required to free it
would take longer than the war's duration,
she had no recourse but to forget it.
When she took the omnibus there, downstairs
she found tables, chairs and curtains missing,
maps strewn on the floor, riding equipment
stacked up in the parlor, empty bottles,
broken china, and a shattered mirror.
Dust accumulated in the corners.
They would not allow her in her bedroom
upstairs, but when she said she'd once lived there,
they obliged her — this she told me later —
offering to let her move in with them.
One room had been converted to their "office"
where, they told her, they "conducted business,"
selling steamers for Ben Butler's brother

to the highest bidders from the north.

Once I learned this, I had all I needed
to recover Bressie's house. I used it.
Not that they would ever be convicted
for embezzlement, nor could I stop them,
but at least my threats forced them to move out
after General Banks's appointment. Butler,
though the Union loved his iron-fisted,
cold and brutal treatment of New Orleans,
finally went too far, filching so much
even Lincoln started hearing of it.
So they shipped him back to Massachusetts
where he ran for governor of Boston.
(Maybe Verdi does know something I don't.)
No one proved him guilty of harrassment,
tampering with funds, nor racketeering
by illegally obtaining dry goods,
private stocks and steamers. This was war time.
Butler had himself announced the order
giving him leave to imprison persons
on suspicion of their clothing, accent,
or associates. He told them, simply,
he was right and Southerners were wrong.
Then he sold New Orleans for a song.

11

Bressie had not mentioned to her father
what she'd left behind in Brashear City.
Since he never asked, she told him nothing.
Nor had he asked how she'd lived those long months.
He asked only of her health, then answered,
"Good! Your health's important. Now I'm happy.
God knows, daughter, I should not have left you,
and I wouldn't have, if I had known then
how long this war would drag on. I had hoped
to retrieve you in a month or two.
I've known Southern people to be stubborn
but this is ridiculous. They *can't* win.
Still, now we're together, and I'm happy."
Chatting like a mockingbird, he kept on,
giving her no chance to put a word in,
let alone explain.

She thought of leaving,
writing him a note the same way he had,
making her way back upriver. Why not?
Wouldn't Trosler still be waiting for her?
Sitting in her father's parlor, she thought,
Why did I not stay there, go with Trosler
off to Mexico, or somewhere further?
Was it wrong to leave? But if I leave here,
it would mean betraying Father. Who knows
what he'd do to find me. Either way,
I am bound to be despised — for nothing.
As she looked around the room, resentment
like the dust that settles under tables
settled in her mind. She stood abruptly,
as though that might shake it off. **For nothing?**
What have I brought on myself for nothing?

Going to the foyer, to a straight chair
(pure mahogany, as I remember)
with its crocheted seat stuffed full of horsehair,
she sat in the modest way she'd sat there
as a child, when awaiting her uncle,
or some other family member, to take her
on a Sunday stroll along the levee
or a day trip to Lake Pontchartrain.
She felt lonely — like the servant's child
she remembered who would sit by idly,
lolling near the fireplace or tapping
both his hands against the windows, waiting
for his mother to sweep up the parlor,
waiting to grow up to be a servant
and be purchased by the highest bidder.
When her company arrived — all bustle,
noise, and promises of entertainment
bursting through the door like a tornado —
she wished they would ask that child along, too
(which, of course, no one would dream of doing),
as though leaving him behind meant leaving
with him all her loneliness, which he'd keep
perfectly in tact till her return.
It's no wonder swimming by herself
meant so much to her. Out in the water
she could hide herself from that black child,
drown his meager humming, make a silence
only she could interrupt.

Tomorrow,
Bressie thought, **I'll leave this house tomorrow.**
Let fidelity bring satisfaction
when felicity cannot.

She sat still,
waiting for someone to interrupt her
as so often one had done before,
treasuring, at last, this hard-earned silence
in her father's house. **For what? For nothing.**
In that small straight chair she started swaying
side to side, inhaling air like water,
soaking in the afternoon, and rocking.
Was it at that moment I came knocking?

12

I inquired after La Rouché —
who he was, why he seemed so undamaged
by the occupation. What I found out,
when I checked, roused my imagination,
as I thought of Bressie, living alone,
subject to the whims of General Butler
and his staff, whom I knew well, knew *too* well,
since I had to work with them:
All hoodoo:
terrorizing people, cutting lives short
with their rash, incompetent decisions,
damning families to poverty,
poverty that may survive for decades.
Often they would hurry through their files
after sunset, while the building darkened
and, for others, taverns opened. Hoodoo
in the costume of democracy.
Salt thrown in the faces of the conquered.
This may be the New World, one that smothers,
rather than destroys, its enemies,
damning them to rank obscurity,
losing them in file folders somewhere
stashed away in Washington, black magic
of the slow, disintegrating kind,
papers chewed to dust unless some stranger,
strangely moved by strange compassion, finds them.

That is how I felt for Bressie — strangely,
inexplicably compassionate,
even from the first. I can't say why, though.
Maybe it was my own fear of dying
undiscovered. Maybe I felt something
of what she felt, having lost her father
suddenly, as I had as a child
when my father left us. He went westward,
saying he would come and fetch us later,
and, save one brief letter, disappeared.
(Also, there were rumors of a murder
he supposedly committed somewhere —
Iowa or California. Not now.
That's another story.) Maybe I was,
unconsciously, thinking of my own past
and that girl I knew in Philadelphia —
she who taught me love means nothing, she who
when I walked in on her with another
swore she loved me, she whom I came down here
to forget, and who is now forgotten.

Who would pay attention to this woman,
if not me? Is that what I was thinking?
Vanity.

Assuming it was proper —
and protected by the General Order
(23) that women must be civil
to all Northern officers, I stopped by
at the residence on Hospital
on the premise I might find the doctor —
yet I timed it so he might not be there.
I decided I had nothing to lose;
that's precisely what I lost there, nothing.
O how rare and fortunate it is
when your unrealistic expectations
match exactly what you find, like Moses
casually thinking, **If this sea parts,
we shall walk across it**, and the sea parts!
At which point he saunters nonchalantly,
gaping Israelites tagging behind him.

When I knocked and Bressie answered, she stood
bathed white by the mid-November sunlight,
both eyes clear as crystals, energetic,

eyebrows dark, extended cross her forehead,
hair down to her shoulders, in a white dress
which her father'd brought her from New Haven.
It was gathered at the waist, with ruffles
on the shoulders — though it seemed too small,
just a little, and was somewhat dated.
Still she blossomed in it, like a flower
that surprises you in autumn.

"Captain.
What a nice surprise," she said, "Come in, please."

Was she covering some indiscretion
I had inadvertently walked into?
Or was she as lonely as I'd hoped for?
Surely, I did not deserve this pleasure —
to be greeted by this lovely stranger
as though she'd been waiting for me. Later
after she had brought us tea, then dinner,
then a sweet array of cakes and pastries
(which I would describe for you in detail,
were it not late), after we had lingered,
after talking with her until twilight
on the balcony upstairs, I wondered
why I'd been suspicious in the first place.
It had been too long since I'd remembered
people can be kind to one another.
Was it my compassion that had brought me,
or my need for hers? I thought I'd gone there
on the premise I might offer friendship —
and when it came down to it, I offered
what I could: to have her house vacated,
keeping it from Butler's beastly clutches,
then to track her servant, Alexander.
But compared to that which Bressie gave me
these were nothing. She gave me her passion,
her attention, and her independence,
things I'd longed for in myself. She listened
when I talked, as though what I said mattered,
even when *I* knew it didn't. Lively
yet composed, she seemed to have an answer
or a question for my every comment,
as though she had thought the same things earlier
in some other place. We got on so well
no explaining can explain it; only

hints and guesses, these are:
Things were perfect!
Summer had been lifted for the last time.
I was not expected until Friday
back in Thibodaux; today was Tuesday.
Dr. LaRouché was gone the whole day.
No one else stopped by to interrupt us.
She felt rested, though a little bored, too.
I was not what she anticipated
nor was she as self-protective, distant,
and dismissive as I'd feared she might be.
Venus left the house of Mars. And maybe,
maybe, we had come into each other
purposefully, to make peace between us —
she the Creole daughter of New Orleans,
I the errant son of Philadelphia.
We discussed the war, of course. I told her
not about the battle for the bayous,
nor about the number dead and wounded,
but about its likelihood of ending,
always the most arguable topic.
Yet I found in her an ally.
She said,
"Like my father, I believe you *will* win
and will bring an end to slavery soon."

"But?" I asked, expecting her resistance.

"It will cost as much for you in dollars
as it costs us in lives. The wealthy ones,
as they have already, will escape you,
even if they lose their large estates,
while the poor ones you'll convert to your ways —
which, as far as I can tell, aren't better,
no more humane, than ours. You worship money
whereas we believe in form. Or ought to."

"We believe in form," I said, "but money,
well, it reinforces form, supports it
with a backbone."

"Money's an abstraction,"
she replied, her eyes alight with green,
"How you treat a person is what matters,
not how much you pay him. To use money

to rebuild the ethics of a country
I think would be tragic — ”

"But, as you said,"
I broke in, "the rich survive defeat."

"Yes,
but I didn't claim that's how it should be.
Is your goal that everyone be wealthy
or be wise?"

"Or like us, not be either."
She agreed and laughed. A pause descended.
Then I asked her what she thought of Yankees,
if she found us bearable.

She answered,
"Bearable? Not quite. Yet manageable.
You're so impercipient, you Yankees.
You have no idea what you are doing,
like those hordes of locusts that swarm through here
every fifteen years or so. We hate you.
Wouldn't you hate us if we invaded
and evicted you from your own cities?
I'm surprised you ask."

She'd missed my meaning,
obviously. Then she told the story
of the officers who lived in her house.
Later, as the light began to weaken,
I asked her again if she thought Yankees,
some of us, might have our own good reasons
to oppose slave-trading, racketeering,
and the exploitation of the Negroes.
Might not *something* good come of our presence?
She abjured and sighed, "It's so haphazard,
who is saved and who is executed.
Look at me. My father came to 'save' me
but at whose expense?"

"Your father 'saved' you,"
I suggested, "since to leave you stranded
might prove worse than treason. They would kill you
once they learned you were your father's daughter;
we might kill you in the field. He knew that.

And he knows those spies whom Butler traded —
both of whose names start with A — had traced him
and would harm him, if they could. So they're sent
safely out of range, and you come
here, where he can keep his eyes on you.
Things have worked out well. And yet I noticed —
how could I not notice, when I met you? —
you looked so unhappy. What went wrong there?"

Like the evening sky, her color darkened
as she paused to look at me. I wondered
what, if anything, she found in my eyes.
I found everything in hers — my sorrows,
pleasures and ambitions. I said nothing.
Still I felt so comfortable with her,
with the twilight veiling us in shadows,
that it wasn't strange, to wait in silence.

"I would like to tell you. Could you listen?"

"I would try. I want to know about you
more than you may want to tell. It's late, though.
I have stayed too long. I must be leaving.
Might we meet? Perhaps tomorrow evening?"

13

And we met again. And what she told me
I have tried to resurrect these five years,
now and then, in my spare time. She told me
what she wanted me to know and, sometimes,
what she didn't.
So we met the next day
and the next. And every time I met her
we would question, charm and tease each other.
Sitting close to Bressie, I felt settled
like a tree that casts a cooling shadow
on a pond, which then returns the favor
seeping water to the tree's roots.
Later
I demanded her house be evacuated.
She returned to it. Soon I would go there
every chance I had — when I was passing
through the city, carrying a message

from the front lines to the General's office,
or whenever I dreamed up some purpose
to escape the camp in Thibodaux.
I found countless reasons: I was needed
for the stream of paperwork — the files,
inventories and allegiance papers.
Ordering things is something I do well.

Meanwhile, Bressie seemed more comfortable
telling me about what mattered to her,
though she never said that somewhere else
Trosler was still waiting, nor did she say
what she planned to do. But what she told me,
as her intermittent friend, allowed her
to rehearse her thoughts out loud. November,
then December, passed. Then Christmas. New Year's.
January came. Then February.
I began to see her regularly.
I began to want her, too.
It's nothing
when you first desire a woman's body
to accept her beauty and to leave it
to the world. But once you start to know her,
once the commerce of desire increases
in intensity, once what you don't know
becomes not erotic but essential,
not a thing to mingle with but something
you for years have lived without without which,
now that you have savored it, you cannot
choose to live again, a delicacy
deep inside the channels of your own veins —
then desire is everything you're made of.
Once you think of her and, thinking of her,
you no longer think the way you once did,
once her spirit enters in the matter
you have set your mind on, once her body
like an ocean moves in waves toward you
and from yours come elemental surges —
then wanting her changes altogether
as a ripple to a tide.

But, patience.

Trosler, who impatiently had waited
for his own idea of Bressie — ten days,

two weeks, twenty-one days, one month, two months —
slowly lost all hope. His next assignment,
to prepare the bulwarks at Port Hudson,
carried him off further from New Orleans
than before. And Bandeaux was no help,
like a peddler offering diversions,
balms for heartaches, tonics for despondence.
Once near Christmas, thinking of the last year
when at Helen's he had feigned an illness,
Trosler sent again for Bandeaux. **Press him,**
he thought, **and he may come up with something.**
Bandeaux always does.

But Bandeaux didn't.
From the moment he arrived, he grumbled:
"What is one supposed to eat around here?
I've had nothing since my breakfast, nothing,
just one of those dreadful army biscuits.
How do you survive?"

"We're under-rationed,"
Trosler offered, "We survive by spirit.
Tell me. Why have I not heard from Bressie?
What is to be done?"

"I can do nothing.
Not at least until I've had some dinner."
Bandeaux brushed the dust from his lapels,
took his coat off, and sat at the field desk
where they shared a simple meal, while Trosler,
who had had no appetite for weeks now,
talked about his dreams again:

"In one dream
I'm a tiger creeping through the forest.
It is dark. I look for Bressie. Slowly,
as one does in dreams, I prowl. In one grove
where the sun breaks through and lights the clearing,
to my great astonishment, a wild boar,
draped in blue, is lying there with Bressie!
They are curled up on the ground together!
Someone like that boar is stealing Bressie,
stealing her from me like pocket silver.
There's so little time left."

Chewing, Bandeaux,
frowning at his meal of bread and saltpork,
first let Trosler ramble on, then stopped him:
"Haven't I told you already, *mon frère*,
dreams are not to be believed. It's saltpork.
I would say that Charles is that boar
with his arms around his long lost daughter.
Either she is happy to be with him
or she's miserable but can't escape.
Either way, with food like this, no wonder
you hallucinate. I say, forget her."

"How can I forget her?"

"Why not write her?"
Bandeaux said, still chewing, "Have you written
since you parted? Say, have you a brandy?"

"What if what I write is apprehended?"

"Didn't you write me? Just use a false name.
I can carry it for you, tomorrow
or the next day. If you send a token,
she'll know who it's from. You'll get your answer,
one way or the other: If she writes back,
she'll explain the cause of her delay.
If she doesn't, you'll know she has fooled you
and you may as well forget her. Listen,
is there any place for me to nap here?
I'm exhausted."

Trosler took no comfort
in his friend's advice. "You've nothing better?"
he asked. Bandeaux shrugged and started searching
for a handkerchief to blow his nose in.

"What can you expect? Life is a struggle,"
Bandeaux snapped. He lay on Trosler's cot.
Meanwhile Trosler sat and wrote his letter,
this time unassisted by his "better."

14

1863: As I once promised
soon I will describe, as she undresses,
Bressie's beauty. Not that it was perfect
when we first made love — our bodies,
just like any bodies, had their flaws,
joints that ached, declining hips, dark hollows.
But the blending of our conversations
with our long caresses, like an image
merging with ideas, awakened in me
something I had never known. At thirty
you drift in and out of your desire
like a listener lost in an epic.
Waves of lust rush through you and your passion
rises in a frenzy you can't hold to,
sudden sheer delight, a momentary
eloquence you wish would last forever —
comfort, strength, amorphous water, fire.
But as easily as language wanders
into arbitrary meaning, or music
without thought recedes in your reflections,
longing, too, will casually diminish
in an afternoon's pacific breezes
lulling you with their inconstant rhythms.
Lust enjoys this stretch of quiet, sometimes,
when you're thirty. Then to be awakened,
to be shaken back into your senses,
is to be reborn into a new world
more enticing than the old, more fragile
yet more magical, its complications
mixed with wonder, sadness graced with awe.

Over time, when I would visit Bressie
she could stir in me, like something ancient
and forgotten, swimming to the surface,
changes I had not anticipated,
bringing with them clarity, like water
springing from a secret geyser.
This day
I am thinking of, I come to Bressie
as I have before. It's February
but the morning sun is warm and balmy.
I have brought a present. It's a silk scarf
trimmed in lavender and with red flowers

woven on a white and turquoise background.
"Something I found at the market," I say.

Bressie seems delighted: "I can wear it
when I wear my wreath." She runs to get it
but returns with more than just her garland.
"Here. A silver brooch. It was my mother's,"
she says, "I think you should have it, David."

"Bressie!"

"Take it. You don't need to keep it,
not forever. But if you should need it,
you know, as a charm or something, wear it.
It's the only thing I have to give you."

"You don't need to give me — "

"Take it, David."

I look carefully at it, a small rose
delicately lined as nature's own rose,
two leaves, and a silver stem to pin it.

"It is lovely." I say, "Try your scarf on."

"I can't wear this scarf with this old house dress,"
she laughs, gently mocking, "I've a skirt, though,
it will go with perfectly."

"Then wear it,"
I say, pinning her brooch to my collar.

"It's for warmer weather."

"Let's go in, then,"
I suggest, emboldened. What I hope for
I am not exactly sure. She pauses.
Pleasure's the result of many causes.

15

Here, then, near the end is our beginning:
Bressie puts her skirt on, with her new scarf

wrapped around her waist. She is the present
I will open, open. When the time comes,
blithely we ascend the stairs, like angels
on the way to heaven, all the air filled
with our talk (well, mostly my talk) — voices
blending with the curl of restless fingers,
kisses in her hair, the walls and doorways
in her upstairs hall inviting, open,
open when and where we press against them,
she alive to me, beneath my jacket
arms that rise across my back, sharp sunlight
I remember streaking through the windows,
lightening her fallen hair, its color
auburn, which unlike her eyes does not change
on this gentle winter afternoon.

She pulls back a moment. Then my smooth face
buries itself in her neck and shoulder.

"You are special."

"How?" I ask, reluctant
to withdraw my lips.

"You have a future.
No one else I know is like you, David."

"No one else wants you as much as I do,"
I say, as I take her shoulders firmly,
not unkindly, "Which room is your bedroom?"

"David? If my heart is ever willing —
my small heart in tribulation — if it . . .
if it flees this cage — and if those armies
you're so busy with should stop their combat
giving us a chance to choose each other,
and if anyone believes — "

"What is it?"
I ask with impatience, as my hands drop
to the scarf around her waist.

"I can't say,"
she says, "that I love you. Please forgive me."

"What about him? Do you love him?"

"Nothing.
I can't say I do or don't. There's nothing —"

"But ourselves," I say. I take her scarf off.
She begins unbuttoning her blouse,
then says, "This way," as she takes my free hand.
First we sit together on her hope chest
like a wife and husband. Then I kiss her
awkwardly, not knowing how to hold her.
Then we pull each other's boots off,
finally succeeding. Pause for laughter.
She removes her blouse. She's lovely, lovely
with her shoulders bare, her breasts unfettered
in the narrow afternoon whose narrow shadows
veil what they reveal, the paler color
of her waist, the gathers in her skirt there
trailing to the floor. I rise to touch her.
She returns her hands inside my jacket.

"Take this off," she whispers.

"Let me hold you,"
I plead, as I wrap around her, pressing
to her thighs. I lay her on the bed quilt.
She undoes my shirt.

"There is a small hook,"
she says, "Here. Along the side." I find it
and I pull her skirt below her knees.
I remove my regulation trousers,
then I run my hand inside her thighs.

"David?"

I am pulled by two hands upward
and she kisses me below my ear.
Opening my mouth, I listen, listen
to her breathing. She is reaching downward.
I am curling, with my mouth at one breast
and my legs around hers, like a child.
She unravels slightly, then goes softer.
I expand my grasp. I feel her wander
over me with both hands. I engulf her

with my arms, my hands, my legs, my whole mouth.
Like two vines our bodies cling together,
my foot dangling from the bed, her left hand
planting itself in her goosedown pillow,
crumpled to one side.
                                        Is this the picture
I would have you think of when you think of
Davenport and Bressie? Quiet, naked,
confident and kind — despite not knowing
what the other smelled like in the mornings,
nor what each might want for breakfast, details
otherwise forgotten, clothing
we as easily take off and misplace
as a silver brooch or purple scarf
given to us by another? Loving,
which is not the same as love, enfolds us
in ourselves as in another. Lucky
we are, if our selfishness is widened
to include another in our own kind.
Every kindly thing that is, or would be,
knows that very kindness where is best served,
toward which every kindly thing's inclining,
moving for to come to, like a river
winding its long way toward the ocean.
Kindness — which is not the same as *kindly*
or as *kind* — is fuller, vaguer, stranger,
indispensible to the sublime
yet not always proper to it. Open
like a mouth in longing, always changing,
kindness is coincidental, gentle,
various, and unreserved. Like Bressie.
Think of her as this kind: as an eagle
lighting on a nest of twine and feathers,
as the voice we want that will escape us
from our lack of courage, as the other
we are when we are what we desire.
What is madness? Kindness singed by fire?
Lovers who, when loving one another,
burn yet cannot soothe what burns? Strange flooding
over arid land? The swamp one swims in?

        I intended to exonerate her
not with exaltations, not with reasons,
but with all the small things I remember:
We made love one day in February.

Later that same day she read a letter
she'd received before I came to visit
but had not had time to read.

I left her
to return to Thibodaux and Weitzel.
General Banks had ordered our next advance
to the west, to storm the bayou country.
First we were to stage a seige at Bisland,
Mouton's camp. We marched to Brashear City.
With no opposition, it took one day.
March 11th I was ordered back home
to New Orleans, where I spent a week
(during which time I saw Bressie three times).
Then I took a train to Brashear City
where our move to Bisland — not from fighting
but from marching up the Bayou Teche —
took much longer than our side had planned for.
It was April. Summer was returning,
with its rain and Mississippi run-off.
We trudged through the fields the bayou'd flooded
where, instead of butternuts or graycoats,
we encountered thousands of mosquitoes
eager to save their beloved swampland.
My skin, which had lately known such pleasure,
soon broke out from bloody bites and blisters.
Then on April 13th, outside Bisland,
moments after Weitzel's charge was spoken,
I was shot, my left arm seared and broken.

16

Bressie never told me of the letter
Trosler smuggled to her from Port Hudson.
Each time I had talked with her about him
I'd assumed their short affair had ended
that day on the train. And when I'd ask her
what her motivations had been with him,
she'd explain. But had I really listened?
Why could I not understand her longing?
Where is God that one is kept from knowing
by a random shot, a blind unyielding,
or a dive into a wave of silence?
Who now knows the truth that she might tell it

and be vindicated? All I've written
wants to be undone, undone, undone
and evaporate into the sun.

17

Outside Bisland, they surprised us, firing
at the moment we began advancing.
I was slightly wounded. Grazed by grapeshot.
but the unexpected impact knocked me
with such force, I rose and toppled backward
like a tree ripped from it roots and twisted
in a hurricane. I heard a sharp *crack!*
somewhere in my rib cage. Then I fainted.

When I woke, I heard O'Brien's laughter
from behind. "The dance began without us,"
he joked.

I felt pain. My wrist was swollen
like a sausage casing, and my elbow
underneath the blood splotch on the surface
was as black as ash. In falling backwards
I had somehow landed on my musket
which discharged between my arm and torso.
My whole arm was burning up.

"O'Brien?"
I asked, staring at my bloodstained jacket
sticking to my wound, "Can you assist me?
I can walk, if only I could stand up."

"If I could oblige I would — but, well, sir — "

I spun my head around to find him
propped against a tree. One boot was missing.
In its place a knob of charred flesh lay there.

"Their artillery came out of nowhere,
eh, sir?"

Repulsed, I turned my head away.
Then I looked straight at his bloodshot eyes,
streaked from crying. "O my God, O'Brien,"

I gagged.

"I don't care about it," he said,
"Not the foot. But if they cut my leg off,
I'm a goner. Please don't let them." He knew
how the army surgeons operated
when they found infection in the field.
But in such fierce heat, one's chance of living
after surgery, without enough styptics
to stem the bleeding, was one in hundreds.
Not to amputate meant to condemn one
to intolerable pain from gangrene,
but to amputate meant death. The one hope
someone like O'Brien had was getting
to New Orleans, to St. Stephen's Hospital,
before dying first.

I crawled on one arm
to a bush, which I could use for balance,
as I pulled myself up to my knees.

"I'll go find a quartermaster. Stay here,"
I said, as I stood.

"Whatever you say.
Don't feel much like going for a stroll, sir.
'Look for me tomorrow and you'll find me . . .
wiser? Older? Nobler?' What's that line, sir?"
he asked, laughing. But his speech was slurring.
Shots occasionally rang out around us,
coming from the bayou. In that small grove
where we had been ambushed, I saw bodies —
maybe ten in all — splayed out, some living,
most already dead. Between the spruce trees
stretcherbearers suddenly came running
like a host of angels in blue jackets.
One of them approached me.

"That? That's nothing,"
he quipped, tearing off the bits of black cloth
from my wound. "Go on! Back to the wagons!"
Then he disappeared.

I helped O'Brien
flop into a stretcher. Then I left him

for the rear. The pain was quickly spreading
through my shoulder to my chest. I stumbled,
over stumps and fallen branches, to the wagons
where they were dispensing whisky from large flagons.

18

At St. Stephen's Hospital the next day
(I'd spent all night on a train), they cut first
through my jacket, then up to my shoulder.
Then to stop the pain they chloroformed me.
When I woke, they'd dressed my arm. My clothing
had been confiscated, doused, and burned
to prevent disease. Save for the swelling
from my armpit to my fingertips
and the constant medication I took,
I felt almost new. My few possessions —
seegars, coins, a pencil, scraps of paper,
Bressie's silver brooch, my mother's locket —
lay beside me on a tiny table.
I remember thinking, **What are these things,**
these few things that have meant the world to me,
crawling through the fields? Are these my tribute,
my obituary? Through the long hours
staring at that small heap, I decided
once I healed, I would start writing something,
something, anything. **I won't be silenced,**
I repeated to myself, through half-sleep,
half-delirium, **I won't be silenced**.

Later (I don't know how many days passed)
I was well enough to exercise.
Cots of wounded lined the halls and stairways,
every ward and corridor as crowded
as the rings of Dante's hell. Despite this,
this harrowing array of mangled bodies —
everything from heads completely bandaged
to exposed chests, black from being burned through,
open to the air — each ward was quiet.
No one felt an urge to talk or laugh much,
and the groans and sighs, in languid measures,
drifted up into the vast, gray ceiling.

I inquired after poor O'Brien

but the girl (She wasn't more than thirteen,
though her eyebrows joined across her forehead
and her gaunt face looked much older.) told me
no one by that name had been admitted
in at least six days.
"There's no O'Brien,"
she sighed, "not at least among the living.
Some, you know, they die before they tell us
who they are." She tried to smile for me
as though pleading with me to release her
from her desk. I never found O'Brien.

On a scrap of paper I wrote Bressie:

I MUST SEE YOU PLEASE COME SOON
YOURS, DD

which I then entrusted to a freedman
who, since he had nowhere else to go,
lived inside St. Stephen's, looking for work.
For a coin he took my note to Bressie.

She came right away. I started crying,
I was so relieved to see her.

"David,
you don't need to stay here any longer,"
she consoled me, while the other wounded,
turning in their cots, stared at her, sadly,
wistfully, though no one even grumbled.
After I was issued new clothes, I went
one last time to gather my possessions.
That was when I saw the brooch was missing.
Someone stole it! I thought. Then I doubted
whether I had ever really seen it
on my bedstand. Maybe I had dreamt it.
I checked everywhere, but it was not there,
that small talisman that had preserved me.

I felt I should tell her right away.

"What's it matter?" she asked, "You've come through this
with your life." Besides, she had her scarf still.
With her help, I climbed the omnibus steps
and she braced me for the bumpy car ride

to Erato. There she stripped my bandage,
washed me, and re-dressed my arm with clean cloth.
She worked quickly but attended to me
with the delicacy of a lionness
licking clean her mate. I started purring,
coaxing her to take her clothes off.

"Bressie,
I have seen too much of death. I need you."

"What you need is rest," she said, "It's too soon,
too soon."

"But I want you."

"You don't want me.
You want what you think you want. You're tired."
But instead of listening to Bressie,
hearing what she meant — that she was wanting —
I continued pestering her, cooing
steadily, "I want to kiss you. Please. Now."

She gave in. Believe me, I am sorry
I, like Orpheus, refused to trust her
when she'd asked me to. I had to touch her,
taste her, even though I couldn't hear her,
hear the thunder rumbling in the distance,
feel the breezes changing, smell the storm clouds
closing in. Might that have been the moment
Bressie would have broken into someone
other than the woman she was trapped in?
Later, during my recuperation,
I spent nearly every day with Bressie
and we'd talk for hours. But I did not hear.
In her garden, in my small apartment,
during meals, in bed, or outside walking,
I would chatter on — all time escaping
like the pelican I saw my first day
in Louisiana — and her voice flowed
like the river, slowly guiding me
toward the darkness of the open sea.

19

Never having seen their correspondence,
I can only guess what words to Trosler
Bressie wrote. But I'm the arbitrator
in this story, I who passed between them
like the moon between the sun and earth,
I who wish to make my peace and leave here,
I who brought the war. She told me nothing
during my recuperation, nothing
of her links to Trosler since that evening
she last saw him outside Brashear City.
Why could she not trust me? Did she worry
I would turn against her for her secrets?
If she'd told me, how would I have acted?
Would *my* jealousy become betrayal?
I don't like to think so. Any letter
sent clandestinely to Rebel soldiers
was illegal. Had she tried to tell me,
I'd been faced with having to report her.
She spared me from that dilemma. Too bad
I can take no comfort there.
                                        The letters
I have been the least successful finding
are the last ones they wrote to each other.
I've looked for Bandeaux, but he slipped out
like a packrat from a trap, and with him
he took everything that he could manage —
portraits, sketches, bills of sale, and letters,
anything he thought might implicate him
as a Rebel. Some claim he owed money;
others say they heard he'd booked a steamer,
late in '63, for Massachusetts;
others swear he fled to Greece.
                                        "'These painters'"
one man in the new state legislature
who knew Crispus, Bandeaux's servant, told me,
quoting Crispus quoting Bandeaux, "'Painters?
how can they know art until they've seen it
in its native habitat. To Athens!
Rome! *Et to Arcadia I go!*'"
Then he grinned and hurried off
to the voting chamber.
                                        Not that Bandeaux,
really, could have told me whether Trosler

at the end lost confidence in Bressie;
only Trosler knew what Trosler suffered.

To Port Hudson now: Before the seige starts,
he receives two visitors in April —
Helen, who is traveling to Natchez
to escape the Union occupation,
and a spy named Peter Polyphenos.

When he greets her at St. Francisville,
Helen hardly recognizes Trosler.

"Colonel! You're as pale as a petunia
in the winter," she cries, her gloved hand tapping,
lightly, on his cheek.

"I've not been eating,"
he replies, but then he slicks his hair back,
smoothing his pomade.

They speak of Bressie,
whom, as Helen says, "I've not laid eyes on
for at least half of eternity!
Heaven knows what that mad girl is up to!"

Trosler tells her of his dream, the blue one
with the wild boar in it. Helen pauses,
stunned by Trosler's impropriety,
but recovers (quite as she's supposed to)
and, undaunted, offers a suggestion:
"Why not let my Cassie Mae explain it.
She is constantly philosophizing
and interpreting things for her own people.
It runs in their blood, you know." She smiles
one of those dismissive, frigid smiles
Southern women are so famous for.
Then she calls in Cassie Mae, who listens
as he tells his dream again.

Then she says,
"Oo! Ta lawn what dis mean y'all muss lissen
to what ain't in no book, sah. In dem days
long ago when all da eart' was cubbered,
hogs done played wid us, an' we wid hogs, too,
free-like, like we all was happy chillun.

Dare was birds dare. Buttaflies and rabbits.
All dem creechas happy! All da same, too,
cep'n fo dat tiga — he be you, sah.
He done wanna be da king. No tellin'!
Lawd, dat tiga, he done put dat candl'
deep inside dat forest, an' he burn down
all dem trees in dat place, an' dat fire burn
makin' light in dare. An' all dem creechas,
day is runnin' to dat place loose stars,
jumpin' ober one da utter, happy
as day's Jesus chillun. But dat hole burn —
Oo! — dat Satan's hell! So when day gets dare
day sound off an' cry.
Now dat old tiga
he done see dis as his time to grab 'em
and to et'em up. But when he jump — Ooo!
he done falled down in dat hole he done made,
falled to hell. An' when dem creechas see'm
days all quiet-like, cep'n for one fat hog.
He star braggin', 'Lawdy! Lawdy! Lawdy!
Fall down on yo knees and pray to Jesus!
He done save us from dat debil! Praise lawd!'
An' since dat dare day, all's hogs is preechas!"

"I don't get it," Trosler says.

"Don't listen,"
Helen interrupts, "Why, Cassie woman!
Colonel White is your protector!"

"Lawd! Lawd!
I done tole da trood. Das all, Miz Helen.
Das all I knows."

"*Well*, we *must* get going
or we'll never make it there by nightfall.
Please excuse us, Colonel. I'm so happy
we could meet like this, however briefly."

Two days later Peter Polyphenos,
spy, arrives on horseback from New Orleans.
He delivers his report to Trosler
on the size of the Union reinforcements,
heralding bad news. Then, as he's leaving,
he hands Trosler something he has taken

from St. Stephen's Hospital.

"I thought, sir,"
he says through his gritted teeth, "you'd want this.
Doesn't it belong to someone you know?"

Trosler takes the brooch. He starts to rub it
as though that might help it shine.

"I thought, sir,
you might want to know what it was pinned to,"
Peter Polyphenos adds, "I found it
on the collar of a Union jacket.
One arm was cut off. The rest was blood-stained.
Certainly the man is dead. I thought, sir — "

"Thank you. That's all, Mr. Polyphenos,"
Trosler barks.

"Of course. I'm at your service,"
he replies and disappears forever.
Trosler puts his hand inside his jacket
where one button's missing. Then he reaches
underneath his collar to the small brooch
Bressie gave him their first night together,
pinned to his shirt. He can feel its texture,
delicately lined as nature's own rose,
as he presses it against his neck.
Then he sits down.
"I must sleep. I'm weary.
And it's necessary. Necessary."

20

Stacks of notes, descriptions of Port Hudson,
of the deprivation, wounds untreated,
insects, hours crouched by acanthus bushes,
meals of hardtack, coffee, and a seegar
(if, by then, you hadn't smoked your last one),
hording ammunition, bouts of boredom,
nights attempting sleep under the willows,
anger at a random God, confusion
from the lack of any useful patterns,
dread of getting used to this routine

as listless as the air above the river,
patience for fresh bacon, for the sure shot,
searching for the bodies on the white bluffs
hanging over the east bank, while they watched us,
fear, when least expected, when a gun fired
lodging whimsically in someone's gullet,
or the man who nodded off just inches
from me and was shot before he woke
like a sack of salt at target practice.
No one dared to drag him off for two days.
Or those friendly chats across the river
between men who'd tried to shoot each other
moments earlier:
"Damn! That was close, friend!
If I weighed as much as I'm supposed to,
you'd have landed me for certain."

"Thank you!
If I weren't so tired, I could've bagged you
like a rabbit!"

"Hell, then. Quit your hiding.
Step out now and take a bow."

"I can't, sir.
Much as I'm obliged, I'm going to sleep now."

"Sleep? In that case, why not cross to our side?
We have extra sheets and pillows!"

"Thanks, no.
I prefer the stone bench at the barracks."

And there was that moment that I saw him,
Trosler, with his musket pointed at me,
mine at him, a hundred yards between us.
There our stories interlaced, in passing —
union, justice, confidence — a moment
of oblivion between us, nothing
else, no hero, no triumphant nation,
no immortal acts, no famous speeches
but two men who didn't know each other,
each faced with his own obliteration,
each allowing the other longer life.
Trosler dropped his musket; I stood silent,

drenched in sweat; the sunlight on the river
flickered, like a candle on an altar.
There I learned my right to pause, and falter.

21

Whether he was killed deliberately
or, as I'm inclined to think, was wounded
by a random shot and then infected,
no one knows. There's talk around New Orleans
of commemorating him with a plaque
after we shut down the Freedman's Bureau,
but he's one of those Confederate dead
better off remembered by a legend
than a stone.
                    Still, may the ones who praise him
keep in mind that, even though he killed some
in defense of "independence," one day
he let one survive. May they remind us,
when they laud his loyalty and courage,
how susceptible he was — to kindness,
to the gentlenesses of the spirit,
to despair. And when they speak of virtue,
may they not forget that more than cunning
he embraced the need to care. He loved one
in the way he thought it best to love her.
May that not be always held against him.

    Was it fair? For Trosler to be human
meant he risked not always being there.
Leave him alone. Leave him to the air.

22

I have little time before I leave here,
only hours. My orders came last Thursday:

> NO MORE MONEY FOR NEW ORLEANS. CLOSE SHOP
> AND DEPART.

                    But I have much more business
to attend to — claims, complaints, and clients,
ordinary citizens all leading

brief, dramatic lives. These black men
dwell with poverty, not independence,
never mind what Lincoln said. I'm leaving
but I'm leaving incomplete. I leave here
parents who have still not fed their children,
husbands looking for their wives, and children
nameless, homeless, hungry, and forgotten.
And I leave here others — con-men, mostly —
legislators, lawyers, bankers, actors —
those who've won the future. And I leave here,
once again, my self, to find another
in some other history than this one.
This one tires me; I feel old, as useless
as an aging pack mule, still prolonging,
going on. I must get used to leaving.
No one wants me here — not LaRouché,
who's denied me entrance to his office
and his house for months now, who has answered
not one of my letters. Nor the Negroes
I'm supposed to help but who don't trust me.
Nor the white Orleaners, who now hate me.
Nor the Northern businessmen who hope that,
since I don't take bribes, I'll simply vacate.
Nor the doctors, teachers, and reporters,
all whose jobs I complicate. Nor Helen,
even, who considers me too morbid
to assist in relocating Bressie.
Nor my landlord who wants me to move out
so he can raise the rent. Nor the women
at the city library; they like me
but they think I'm slower than a loris.
Nor the grocer. No. Nor Alexander
who thinks, though we share the same convictions,
I look down on him.
                              And you, my reader,
you to whom I leave this testimony,
might you spend a day or two recalling
little things I've said, the way that Bressie,
when we met, took time to listen to me?
Or that legend of the Teche I made up?
I have made these things from sand. I'm leaving.
There's no way to stop myself from grieving.

23

After Vicksburg fell, Port Hudson fell.
I was gone by then. My new assignment:

> REPORT TO THE CUSTOMS HOUSE, NEW ORLEANS.
> BANKS REQUESTS YOUR SKILLS FOR OFFICE DUTY.
> MY CONGRATULATIONS.
> GODFREY WEITZEL

As soon as I could, I went to Bressie,
hoping she'd be glad to see me. Instead,
I found Alexander in her parlor.

"Sah," he said, "my mizzus ain't been so good.
Docta Charls, he say she got da fever
but I don't see how so. She ain't dyin',
she ain't sweatin', she eat fine."

I panicked
and rushed to her bedroom, where I found her
seated in a chair beside her French doors,
open to the balcony. She smiled.

"David?" she asked, "You've been gone for too long.
I've been waiting. Waiting for the future
you're were going to bring me. Now I'm tired."
She stood up, as though to leave.

"But Bressie — "

"Sorry. I must rest now."

"And tomorrow?
Can we meet again then?"

"Come back, David."

All night I was restless. What had happened?
Once my arm had healed, I'd had to leave her,
suddenly, for duty at Port Hudson
late in May. But now it was July.
Something strange, dismal, had overcome her,
something I could only guess at. No one
I have talked with since has ever told me

what, if anything, occurred. I worried,
to myself, that Alexander's manners
were too intimate. No longer her servant,
not since Bayou Teche, why was he with her?

Then I caught myself. **I must help Bressie**,
I decided, as I smoked a seegar,
flicking ashes through my open window,
Someone's holding her against her wishes.
I must get her out. But how? I wondered.
I felt too unwieldy to be useful,
like a mother turtle who is liable,
rather than to hatch her eggs, to crush them.
Bressie yearned for freedom. That much I'd learned.
But I'd also learned, since our invasion,
freedom can't be granted, not like money,
property, or rank. Whatever freedom
she had known she'd taken for herself
and embraced — like rain one lifts one's arms to.
"What can I do?" I asked of the night air,
as I puffed my seegar, not once thinking
I myself must change to keep from sinking.

24

Five days later, once my job was settled,
I went to Erato Street, and this time
Bressie greeted me alone. **Thank goodness!**

"Let's go out," she said. She tried to smile
but she seemed not too enthusiastic
when she took my arms.

"Where to?" I asked her,
thinking, **Why have I not brought a present?**
That would cheer her up. How stupid I was.

"Why not to Lake Pontchartrain?" she offered,
"I know it's a long way off, but, David,
how I long to see the water."

Heartened,
I said, "Good idea! That's what you need now.
Where is Alexander?"

"I'm not certain,"
she said, vaguely. On an omnibus
we rode to Canal, walking through the Quarter,
following the same steps Trosler'd taken
one triumphant morning four years before.
That was on Thanksgiving; it was hot now,
no assuring breezes, only the sun.
She insisted we walk on the right side
of the street and stay within the shadows.
In her cotton waist and skirt (no corset
on this August day), she had a light step,
almost like an angel's, I remember.
When she turned to me, her eyes were gleaming,
hazel, I think. Then I nearly lost her
at the corner of Elysian Fields,
when she ran ahead to catch the streetcar.

"Wait for me!" I cried.

She started laughing,
as she chased the car and jumped aboard it:
"Hurry, David! You don't want to miss this!"

By the time I caught up, my heart pounding,
whether from the heat or from my longing
I couldn't tell, everything seemed better,
to be sitting with my arm around her,
our first trip together since our long ride
months before from Thibodaux. The motion,
side to side, nudged us against each other,
so she dropped her head onto my shoulder,
singing, "*Ombre légère qui suis mes pas*,"
quietly, to herself.

I would tell you,
if I could, what sweet dreams filled my hopes then,
but I can't. The afternoon is fading.
I've too little time, and I'm forgetting.
Someone's knocking at the door, it's late,
there's a steamer sailing north tomorrow —
I must give her up. Still, I felt panic,
all was *sauve qui peu . . .*

All right! I'm coming!
I remember Bressie humming.

25

While I watched, she walked down to the shoreline,
lifting up her skirt, as though removing
from a lover's corpse his cerecloth, gently,
inch by inch, her fingers gathering it
to her hips, exposing first her ankles,
then her calves, as white as alabaster,
then her knees. She stepped into the water.
Then she waded further out, her long skirt
bunched now in her forearms like a basket,
both her thighs bare, giving back the sunlight,
beads of water glistening there, her strong legs
parting, slightly, while she paused a moment,
shaking out her hair. She threw her head back,
looking at the sky for supplication,
as though waiting for her body to rise.
Then she hitched her skirt up further, further,
and devised it so it wouldn't scatter.
She knew I was watching. Raised still further,
her skirt hung to one side in a bundle,
looking, from that distancc, likc a lotus,
as she waded further still. She reached down,
stretched both hands, and touched the waveless water,
skimming both her palms across its surface,
dipping her fingers in. Then, with hands cupped
in a silent ritual, a baptism,
she scooped a handful of water above her,
watching as it spilled onto her forehead,
crystal droplets, luminous as silver.
Finally, she dipped her hands back downward,
splashing water on her face, her head bent,
eyes hidden in the gesture of one crying,
palms pressed to her cheeks, neck bare, hair matted,
as the water dripped onto her breasts,
wetting her blouse. Then she pulled her hands back,
suddenly, and wiped them on her skirt.
She glanced at me, and I started to smile,
but, just as I thought she was returning,
like a gull in one glide she dove in
and was gone. The world began to spin.

26

Here's the telling only. Have I told you
matters separate from what really matters?
But what matters matters unremembered,
isn't that so? Is God here? Do you know?
What's important isn't that I saved her,
though to say that now seems strange: *I saved her!*
I saved her from drowning! I saved Bressie!

I yanked off my boots and ran toward her,
splashing through the shallows. Then I fell down,
tripping over some branch underneath me.
After I stood up, I started calling,
"Bressie!" Reaching down, I tried to grab her
without diving straight into the water.
I remember thinking, **It's much colder,**
colder and darker than it seemed from shore.
Sauve qui peu! as I continued coaxing,
"Come on out now! Stop this teasing, Bressie.
I know where you're hiding. Stop now."

Silence,
save the sound of the water lapping, lightly,
on my shoulders.
Once my mind took over,
I inhaled as deeply as I could,
then dove under, arms spread out, eyes open,
legs apart and kicking. Enough sunlight,
breaking through the surface, helped me see
but below me all I saw were shadows,
none distinct enough to be a body.
Pushing with what strength my panic gave me,
I shoved to the bottom, arms flung forward,
and made systematic sweeping motions.
Soon, in need of air and losing depth,
I began to surface. Then I touched her,
feeling bare flesh swipe my hand. I surfaced,
sucked in all the fresh air I could manage,
and dove down again. This time I saw her,
clear as though she were beneath a full moon,
hair spread in an arc around her pale face
but without the wreath she had been wearing,
her skirt torn away, her white blouse weightless
as it rose and left her body naked,

bare legs stretched apart. She slowly swiveled
to the side, beginning to rise, lengthwise,
so I grabbed her thighs and jerked them downward.
Then I slid my hands up to her hips
and began to push her. I felt something,
gratefully — a rock or stump below me
I could use for leverage. A hard ache
filled my throat, now panicking for more air,
as I whipped my neck and leaned toward Bressie,
pushed my head into her naked stomach,
sucked and thrust and heaved until, together,
we broke through the surface. As I inhaled,
I sucked in so hard I started choking.
Then I heard her coughing, too. A few yards
from us the lake was shallow. Delicately,
like a groom leading a highstrung racehorse,
I tugged her arm and eased toward the shore.
She kept coughing, spitting gobs of water,
eyelids stained by plastered strands of wet hair.
As I pulled, I sensed her looking at me.
Then we reached a spot where I could stand
so I slipped my hands beneath to guide her
back to land. Still retching, clinging to me,
she attempted to avert her head,
pulling toward the lake. I held her closer,
as when making love, and waded slowly,
lifting her into my arms, out of the water,
hoping I might take her all inside me.
But her body was too soaked and heavy
like a sack of salt or cannon powder
left out in the rain. I couldn't hold her.
I began to cry.
                        I laid us both down
at the water's edge. She started panting,
so I started panting with her, loudly,
trying to create a steady rhythm
both of us could follow, then ease up from.
How long we lay in the mud I don't know,
panting heavily in broken rhythms.
As I stared up at the empty sunlight,
I could hear her next to me, still panting,
but I didn't touch her.

                              Then a shadow,
in the corner of my eye, came closer,

howled, and ran off. Reaching out toward her,
I felt the sand sticking to her shoulder.

"Find a doctor," I said. She said nothing
but just lay there, breathing heavily.

I repeated, "I'll go find a doctor."
She sat up, as though my voice had shocked her,
then faced the last one she had put her hope in,
staring through me, both dark eyes wide open.

27

Memory is only what we make it.
Who was faithless? Who's gone mad? Who suffered?
Who saved whom? Why can't I stop?
No matter.
I go on, go on. Still, Bressie's missing.
Why is it no one will let me see her?
Alexander they allow to visit
but he has no answers for my questions —
neither true nor false, no glimpse, no reason
why she will not speak. So can it matter
that I "saved" her? "Saved" her? "Saved" her for what?
For her father's kindness, or his torture?
"Saved" her *from* what? From my own betrayal?

Maybe. Would I have kept pressing this long,
had they not kept Bressie from me? Maybe.
Maybe she was carrying our child
when they took her in that day and held me
on some minor charge. But two days later,
they released me when she wouldn't tell them
whether I'd tried to strangle, rape or drown her.
Maybe Bressie's dead and they won't tell me.
Maybe they themselves cannot accept it.
Maybe she has told them what they wanted.

But from what I gather, she's said nothing,
nothing, nothing, nothing, nothing, nothing.
Had they any choice but to release me?

I go on, go on, as though the answer
lay in what I know — or what I have known.

It's kept me from completing anything.
Yet after five years, I still know nothing,
and what matters changes. So I'll stop now.
I'll go north tomorrow, to a people
who believe in progress, not in faith,
leave behind these pages, and bequeath them
to this fettered place that has no future.
I concede now I have got things all wrong,
making up what's faded, what's remembered
bent, like light refracted through a prism.
Here it is (I hear the steamer whistle!) . . .
Here it is, this small wave rolling toward you.
Trust me, reader. Though I am not honest
I can sense another wave behind this.
I leave you the telling, should you find this,
you who know best how to measure kindness.

The author thanks the University of New Orleans for several Faculty Summer Scholar Awards, a College of Liberal Arts Stipend, and sabbatical leave time during which much of this book was developed and written. He also wishes to acknowledge the National Endowment for the Arts for a Creative Writing Fellowship that allowed substantial time for revisions at a later stage. In addition, he expresses deep appreciation to readers who provided feedback on all or parts of this poem — in particular to: Rick Barton, Mackie J-V. Blanton, John Cooke, Mary de Rachewiltz, Joy Desforges, Kathleen Diffley, Alfred Dorn, Barbara Eckstein, Dana Gioia, Gunesh Gery, John Hazlett, Cynthia Hogue, Carl Malmgren, Robert McPhillips, Biljana D. Obradovic, Hildegard Sandhusen, J.P. Travis, Frederick Turner, Tom Whalen, Laurie A. Williams, Sonny Williams, and Anne Prouty.

John Gery is a Research Professor of English at the University of New Orleans. He has served as Director of the Ezra Pound Center for Literature at Brunnenburg Castle, Italy, since 1990. His previous collections of poetry include: *Charlemagne: A Song of Gestures* (Plumbers Ink), *The Enemies of Leisure* (Story Line), and *American Ghost* (Raska Skola & Cross Cultural). He is also the author of a critical study, *Nuclear Annihilation and Contemporary American Poetry: Ways of Nothingness* (Florida). His poetry, criticism and reviews have appeared in *American Literature*, *Chicago Review*, *George Washington Review*, *Kenyon Review*, *The Iowa Review*, *Louisiana Literature*, *New Orleans Review*, *Notre Dame Review*, *Paris Review*, *Poet Lore*, *Southwest Review*, and *Verse*. He has received awards from the Academy of American Poets, the National Endowment for the Arts, the Louisiana Division of the Arts, and Deep South Writers.